MODEL RAILWAY

Layout, Construction and Design Techniques

MODEL RAILWAY

Layout, Construction and Design Techniques

Nigel Burkin

THE CROWOOD PRESS

First published in 2010 by
The Crowood Press Ltd
Ramsbury, Marlborough
Wiltshire SN8 2HR

www.crowood.com

British Library Cataloguing-in-Publication Data
A catalogue record for this book is available from the
British Library.

ISBN 978 1 84797 181 4

ACKNOWLEDGEMENTS

During the planning and building of this layout, the comments
and suggestions of my friends and fellow operators have been
of great help. I would like to thank Graeme Elgar and Eddie
Reffin for their invaluable input that helped shape my efforts.

I would like to acknowledge the assistance of David Jones
of Dapol, Dennis Lovett of Bachmann Europe plc and Simon
Kohler of Hornby for their practical assistance and for allowing me access to new developments. To Jon Jewitt of Sun-
ningwell Command Control, together with Digitrax for their
assistance with DCC control equipment, which has been used
on the MRL N scale layout project. I would also like to thank
Alan Murray, formerly of MacKay Models of Paisley, for his
support and assistance with Lenz equipment, used on the
top deck project.

Research is an important part of creating such layouts. I
would not have managed without the assistance of many
people at Montana Rail Link. They gave me a great deal of
help with information, documents on operations and access
to the property. I would like to give special thanks to Pete
Lawrenson, Chief of Safety and Security, for his kind assistance and his wife Pat Lawrenson, for her kind hospitality
during our field trip.

Finally, and not least, I dedicate this book to my ever sup-
portive wife Sarah, who helped me to build the log cabin
that houses the layout. Without her help and determination,
6.5 tons of white cedar would still be lying on the drive!

Typeset by Shane O'Dwyer

Printed and bound in Malaysia by Times Offset (M) Sdn Bhd

CONTENTS

INTRODUCTION

Layout building is exciting, rewarding and perhaps the most challenging part of being involved with model railways. A layout provides a home for our enthusiastically acquired collections of locomotives and rolling stock, becomes a centrepiece we can show to visitors and is an important statement about our creativity too. For many, it provides vital escapism and relaxation in an increasingly stressful world of work. Other modellers use it to transport them back to golden eras remembered from childhood or to model an 'ideal world', far removed from reality. Modellers living in urban areas can create miles of idyllic open country in a basement or loft or, in my case, the mountains of Montana in 1:160 scale, in an outbuilding situated in

Freight traffic has grown on the British rail network in the last ten years. One location that has benefited from the traffic boom, especially in intermodal containers, is Grangemouth in central Scotland. Traffic of a variety of types, in specialized containers, works in and out of this port location, including supermarket traffic. EWS Class 66, No.66099 departed for Mossend and Trafford Park with a service destined ultimately for Europe via the Channel Tunnel on 21 May 2009. Every intermodal unit on that train was a specialized tank of some description, there being no traditional boxes loaded. The location also sees petroleum traffic from the nearby refinery and container traffic from the port itself, which is located further down the line seen in this photograph. That and some very interesting semaphore signals make it a perfect theme for a layout.

the Scottish Highlands nearly 5,300 miles away from the full size railroad. The social side of the hobby should not be forgotten, and many modellers working on home layouts enjoy the companionship and support of close friends during construction work parties and operating sessions. There is no doubt that the hobby brings benefits and comfort to many people.

During my time in the world of corporate work, railway modelling offered escapism and a way to relax, both on my own as a 'lone-wolf' modeller and with friends too. Doing something creative and practical with my hands clears my mind and helps to put things into perspective. If, at the same time, I create a length of the Kent coast main line in 4mm scale, that's also a very good thing.

The benefits of building a model railway are many, and, over the years, I have found myself travelling to places many hundreds and sometimes thousands of miles from home, on exciting trips to explore and research railways around the world, with layout construction and design in mind; meeting many interesting people in the process and learning a great deal about the many and varied approaches to the hobby, and real life railroading. These experiences would not have been gained from a typical package holiday, but planning them is an interesting step outside the norm, which has broadened my horizons and resulted in long-lasting friendships too.

Building a layout also allows me to practise different skills such as joinery (not cabinet-grade joinery, I hasten to add), track building, layout planning, electronics and landscape creation to mention a few. My imagination plays a key role in helping me to visualize a model railway concept; hours of day dreaming have saved me from insanity in a variety of repetitive and boring work meetings over the years. Doodling track plans is the purpose for which notepads were designed, not taking the minutes. Research can provide the inspiration and drive to create something in whatever available space can be found in the family home. There is a great deal of satisfaction in discovering the ideal location upon which to base a layout theme which will fit a given situation and then having the fun of working out the track formation, discovering the traffic which was operated over the line, and even arranging

a field trip to see what remains, to take photographs and make notes as far as possible. A great excuse for a day out!

A fully finished and successful layout has to be the ultimate goal for a modeller. There is little doubt that it will be biggest and most significant investment in time and money any modeller can make and, make no mistake about it – a layout can gobble up a great deal of both, which is why it is so important to get things right, most if not all the time.

A warning: this is not a book of sterile techniques, describing in cold detail the different ways to build a baseboard or two – that's been done many times before. All I would be doing is repeating such techniques if this book were presented in such a way. Instead, it demonstrates how I filled a 360sq.ft log cabin with the all-important skeleton of a complex model railway, building it from the ground up to the point that trains were running reliably using Digital Command Control systems.

On the way, I used several techniques to achieve my goal and I will state up front that there is nothing unique about any of them, they have all been tried and tested in one form or another before by other modellers, either here or abroad. The point is how to use these methods to make the best of my position and to achieve my railway modelling goals, not to introduce new and far-flung ideas that would be hard for anyone to replicate.

All of the ideas, experiences and lessons learned from making mistakes (as few as possible) described here can be applied to any model railway project. I take the modeller from floor level to finished bench work with track, wiring and running trains, together with thoughts on how I planned the layout and decided upon construction methods. There is nothing 'finescale' about my approach, nor do I sit on some high plateau of purist techniques using hard to find materials. Instead, I used basic power tools, broke my share of drill bits, cut myself about a dozen times, removed several hundred splinters and swore a great deal too. The 'layout' is now structurally complete, as far as the scenery and presentation finishing stage, which is an entire subject on its own and deserving of a separate book. Alas, a lack of space here prevents me from describing the fascinating art of modelling specific structures, infrastructure, scenery, mountains, rivers and trees.

My 360sq.ft is not a great deal of space when compared to some truly enormous basement or museum layouts built by modellers in the United States and Europe, but is still a sizeable commitment when matched with what can be achieved in the average home in the UK or apartment living in a North American city. I use techniques to increase the available real estate in the cabin so I could have long main line runs, 10ft long trains in N scale, and still leave room for a couple of comfortable chairs, my modelling work bench and storage. In designing the layout many influencing factors had to be taken into consideration, and my experiences show that it is possible to have your cake and eat it too, with some careful planning. So, you won't find a book of track plans, but valuable layout-design ideas on making more room for track, scenery and buildings, together with allowances for human beings too. I look at quick ways of constructing layouts and how I decided upon construction methods from the many available to us.

A BRIEF NOTE ON TERMINOLOGY

I model both British and North American railways, which have different terminologies for full-size features and in layout construction. I freely interchange these terms within the book. A railway in the United Kingdom is also called a 'road' or 'rail road' in the US. Baseboards in the UK are called bench work and layout tables by our fellow American modellers. Track bed or road bed: which is it? They are both the same. Masonite or hardboard; freight cars or freight wagons; back scenes or back drops; latex paint or emulsion paint, they are broadly the same. Passing loops on a British railway would be called a 'siding' or 'passing siding' on a North American railroad. Sidings in the UK are just that, while in North America they may be called a stub track, spurs or something similar. A railway station in the UK is a passenger 'depot' on the opposite side of the Atlantic. I trust that the terminology is self-explanatory and in no way an attempt to introduce American terminology to British operations and vice versa. But one term you won't find beyond this introduction is 'train station'. Yeuch!

OPPOSITE PAGE:

TOP: *Time travel is possible with a model railway. Steam-era railways can be modelled using a huge variety of hi-fidelity ready-to-run products, and both the locomotive types shown in this picture are available in 4mm scale. The preservation scene is also popular, offering the chance to mix a variety of locomotives in one model which otherwise may never have been seen together in the past.*

BOTTOM: *Capturing the action in miniature is the driving force behind the construction of a model railway layout, and scenes like this taken at Sandpoint, Idaho can set the pulse racing. However, you need a great deal of space to model freight trains of this size and the choice of scale is an important factor when making planning and design decisions about train length and the landscape surrounding the railway itself. BNSF 5316, a C44-9W leads an SD40-2 with a lengthy train of auto-rack cars west towards Spokane on 4 July 2007.*

A NOTE ON PHOTOGRAPHY

Layouts are large structures and, as construction of my projects progressed, space to set up lights and a tripod became ever more restricted. A very wide angle lens was used to get everything into each shot, with unavoidable lens distortion of some of the images. Please bear this in mind when studying the joinery techniques – my joints are square, believe me, or the layout would not work.

THE LAYOUTS WITHIN THE MULTI-DECK PROJECT DESCRIBED

For clarification, and because this is a complex project, there are three layout themes accommodated on the multi-deck layout concept described here. One

I have been fascinated by the railways of south-east England since I became aware of the hobby. Apart from my US railroading interests, the former South-Eastern Division of the Southern Region of British Rail, together with its third rail electrification, has had a strong attraction for me. This is the classic view of Ramsgate depot photographed in May 2009, inhabited by 'Electrostar' units these days. It makes an excellent layout design element, and its slam door EMUs may be long gone but not forgotten in my world of railway modelling, as you will soon see.

is an American N scale theme based on the Montana Rail Link. It is referred to as the MRL N scale layout and occupies the lower two of the three decks of the layout.

The top deck is designed to accommodate two layouts, the scenic parts on either side of a double-sided back drop. One is a British outline 4mm-scale theme and is referred to as 'Folkestone East', a location on the Kent coast main line. I originally planned to build a piece of Redhill, Surrey on those boards, but re-evaluated that during the design stage. The other theme is planned to be North American HO, with the location undecided upon when work on the layout was started.

SO TO WORK

There's a layout cabin to fill, piles of timber lying around waiting to be sawn into L-girders, sub-track (road) bed, a helix to build and trains to put to work. I planned to complete the basic structure or skeleton of the layout with some measure of operation in around fourteen months. I hope you enjoy this journey of model railway layout construction as much as I did. If it succeeds in helping you with ideas for your grand design, even in . a small way, I shall be nothing less than delighted.

CHAPTER ONE

DEVELOPING A THEME AND FINDING SOME SPACE

Before plans for a grand design layout could be formulated I relied on short, end-to-end linear layout concepts, such as this one based on operations from the two suburban platforms at Reading General Station. Named Platforms 4a and 4b, the layout allowed for large station operations in a compact area. The theme involved modelling just part of the station, together with features suggesting a much larger railway site in EM gauge and representing the British Rail-privatization transition period.

INTRODUCTION

Ideally, before getting down to detailed layout design, the modeller should develop a theme for the planned layout. In my case, a handful of themes were rattling about in my head for consideration, and prototype information for many of them literally overflows out of box files ready for use when I had finally settled on one of them.

Furthermore, a home has to be found for the layout and decisions taken regarding the type of layout concept that will suit the given space, for all these things are linked together. There is a lot of thinking and planning to do, and the available space, time and resources will have a bearing on the preferred theme and the layout concept too. Undertaking a layout that will bust the budget in planed timber alone is not going to achieve anyone's objectives, nor is working on a theme that will not suit the available space.

I spent hours giving consideration to the ideal theme to suit my space. Developing a theme is quite different

from practical track planning and layout design which are covered in the next chapter. A specially constructed outbuilding was left standing for eighteen months before I made any move to build the first baseboard for the grand project. Yes, a couple of small portable layouts took up residence and were worked on in that intervening time, but no progress was made on anything more permanent. The reason was simple: I was mulling over themes and concepts, together with thoughts on how to squeeze as much as I could into the available space without impacting on the atmosphere of this particular building. I had quite ambitious plans to scratch a number of modelling itches more or less at the same time and being able to do that was always going to be a challenge.

Finding some real estate for our railway empires is challenging for most of us, and sometimes the only option is for the layout to occupy family space in the home. That space may be found in a basement, which also serves as a hobby and recreational area, together with space for practical household things such as

BELOW: Space will always be an issue for all modellers, no matter what company or era that they model. One way of developing a theme for a model that might not take up too much room is to look for secondary passenger operations that may rely on short train formations hauled by popular classes, such as the Class 37

powered train, seen in this June 2004 picture of EWS Class 37, No. 37411. An alternative is to explore the available two- and three-car multiple units such as the Class 150s recently released by Bachmann in 2009. The train in this picture, which was taken at Carlisle, consists of four coaches and a locomotive at either end, in what is known as 'Top and Tail' mode. Even in 4mm-scale, this would result in a model nearly 6ft in length.

LEFT: A possible layout theme: the Kent coast, on the electrified line between Ashford and Dover in the privatization transition era, modelled to 4mm scale, EM gauge. I like early summer as a season for this theme and placing it across the time interval between the construction of the Channel Tunnel and around New Year 2000. This would provide a home for my collection of third rail electric 'slam-door' multiple units and stretch the time era over about nine years, providing a great deal of interest.

freezers, washing machines, heating systems and storage. Likewise, the use of a spare bedroom or space in a study or other room in the house means that the layout concept must be considered with care. How will the physical construction of an often large, wooden structure impact on the immediate surroundings?

Take a look at the alternatives for housing a layout to which I gave serious consideration: garages are a better option than bedrooms when considering the possible construction mess, but also have to serve other purposes such as storing cars, boats and bicycles – a most strange use for a garage indeed, I hear you say. Sheds, outbuildings and cabins (like my layout space) all offer possibilities and all have advantages and disadvantages of their own. Lofts are frequently chosen for accommodating a layout, but access may be problematic. How will all of this affect your grand design? Let's take a look at possible layout sites before developing the layout concept.

One of my druthers for a Kent coast theme would be the South-East Travelling Post Office (TPO) service and the earlier Dover–Manchester TPO service. This view shows the South-East TPO at Dover with Class 73 Electro diesel locomotives in charge.

This may be typical of the loft space found in many homes. This loft of mine is dusty with little useful headroom. The pitch of the roof makes much of the space unusable anyway, and equipment such as water tanks, electrical cables and the inverter for solar PV panels may have to be relocated at a significant cost.

FAR LEFT: Should your layout space be less than perfect, you can overcome some problems with technology: a dehumidifier is a useful device for areas that are relatively damp, such as basements or outbuildings, of which garages are an obvious example.

LEFT: Rodents are a real nuisance – they eat through cables and damage valuable models. Deter them with ultrasonic devices that are cheap to buy and run. This one is used to protect the contents of my loft and simply plugs into a wall socket.

FINDING A HOME FOR THE LAYOUT

SPARE ROOM

Space in the house is perhaps the hardest thing to dedicate to a layout, unless a spare bedroom is available after the offspring have left home, or a larger house than was needed for the immediate family has been purchased. House room is great for several reasons, including the benefit of good heating as part of the home central heating system. It is secure within brick (or stone) walls with easy access, a power supply will be readily available and a degree of comfort can be enjoyed in the home, which may not be possible with remote sites. After all, the bathroom is probably just down the hall and the kitchen (with important things like the kettle and fridge) nearby.

So why are spare rooms rarely taken up as an option? If my spare room is anything to go by, I could not use the space efficiently. Covering over the window is not an option and having to make allowances for an inwardly opening door (sometimes the door can be rehung, but not always) reduces the quality space for a layout. Furthermore, allowances made for other family members may result in the smallest room only being available and that could be a miserly 10ft by 8ft, or thereabouts. Could you work your grand design into that space without resorting to a very complex piece of joinery and making massive compromises? Also, consider tramping through the house and up the stairs with sheets of plywood, planed timber and other sheet materials. Where are you going to be able to cut them without the resulting mess affecting the adjacent living space? I rejected my spare room for that reason alone – the mess would be difficult to control and tramping in and out every time I needed to cut and smooth wood was going to be a pain. A solution would be to have material sawn to the required specifications by the timber merchant, but that would add to the budget for materials.

As an aside, those modellers with young families have found that the imminent arrival of another child soon puts pressure on domestic living space such as spare bedrooms, and layouts soon take on the appearance of an unnecessary luxury. A lot of hard work could be lost if the room were no longer available. This is where portable layouts have a role to play as a way of enjoying a layout and yet reducing the impact on the domestic arrangements.

Shelf layouts have grown in popularity for those accommodated in the home because they can be attached to a wall with minimal disruption to the rest of the room, especially at a height of around 60in from the floor. Studies and home offices have been known to house small, linear shelf layouts located over the desk or across filing cabinets. Be sure that you do not disrupt normal work activity, and the comfort of operations is also a consideration. It is generally accepted that space should be dedicated to the layout where it does not impact on other household activities. That definitely rules out the kitchen.

CELLARS AND BASEMENTS

If you are fortunate enough to own a house with a cellar or basement (there is a mistaken belief among some modellers in the UK that all homes in the United States have basements) the almost ideal space exists for a layout. The advantages include good security within the home, together with an immediate power supply and probably good access from the living space too. How usable that space turns out to be depends on the design of the home and the services located in the basement, such as heaters, air conditioning and water purification units. Will load-bearing walls divide up the space, creating impenetrable barriers to the construction of the scale permanent way?

I lived in Europe for many years during my childhood and remember homes in Germany with large cellars: dry, clean and with good access from the outside, as well as through the kitchen. Ideal space, you might think. Surprisingly, it was not. The ceilings were low and the space divided up into too many small rooms for utility purposes. When considering a cellar you do need to consider damp-proofing too, and whether the space is accessible enough to bring in layout building materials. Can the space be transformed from a bare brick or block-walled utility space into somewhere pleasant enough to spend time with friends?

ATTICS AND LOFTS

No cellar and no spare bedroom? What's next? Oh yes, the loft – that space occupied by spiders, dust, insulation and tinkling header tanks for vented central heating systems. Despite all that, it is space and within the security of the house too. But is it suitable for a layout?

Space is always available in a loft and it can be good quality space, depending on the build of the house. I looked at the loft in my cottage and, while it offered over 30ft by 18ft in the main area over the living room, there was very little head room and, as the pitched roof runs down to the walls, that height problem is made a great deal worse. The only truly usable area was 30ft by about 6ft, if I were to keep my head from hitting roofing timbers. The area was claustrophobic and unpleasant. Not ideal, even assuming that I could clad the outer roof area, insulate it against heat, cold and dust and that I could enlarge the very small access hatch.

This underlines the problems with loft space in most houses, yet I know a friend with a lovely 14ft square loft, which he is happily filling with a British outline N gauge layout. Even he has had a few near misses with the loft hatch, and that is with a purpose-built loft ladder! Climbing in and out of lofts is a pain and that could be a factor for modellers past retirement age where mobility is not what it used to be.

Lofts in modern houses have a great deal more timber in them as thinner A-frames are used to hold the roof up. Such structural members get in the way of layout construction and cannot be modified without affecting the structure of the house and its roof. Loft conversions are expensive, but will deliver some valuable quality space. You will need planning permission for such conversions in the UK, the work would have to be properly assessed by a structural engineer and carried out by a competent builder with good references.

The temptation to lay down flooring boards over the insulation in modern houses and to string baseboards along the roof timbers is strong for many and that, together with some wiring work, insulation, painting and other improvements will deliver valuable space, and probably for a reasonable price. However, be aware that some modern houses do not have particularly strong roof spaces: it is enough to hold the roof up in the severest weather, but that's it. Introduce a lot of

modelling equipment, beer and some men playing trains and something might give. Check the specifications of your home and also the warranties before going too far down this route.

Older properties may have roof space already converted as living space such as former servants' quarters – ideal space, except that it may be divided up into small rooms and with narrow access stairs. When buying a house, look for space for your layout and consider every option. If an older house suits, the roof space may be structurally stronger and more suitable than with a newer house. However, in my case that was not to be, and the added problems of a loft hatch and of dragging materials through the house ruled it out for me.

GARAGES

While being a good place for dealing with the inevitable mess that results from layout building and having with lots of room, a garage is generally draughty and damp, especially if it is used to store a car. Hard concrete floors make it uncomfortable for working on the layout for extended periods and the large door can make insulation difficult. I calculated that converting a garage for layout use would cost the same as an outbuilding or a bespoke cabin. By the time the large doors were made secure, the area insulated and draught-proofed, the costs make the garage an unattractive option. Also, check that the floor is level and even.

On the plus side is the large space made available, and perhaps buying a really good quality wooden garage and converting it for use as a home for a layout may be an option for you to consider. However, if you intend spending the money on something like that, why not go for a machined log cabin, loft conversion or a really good quality garden shed?

SHEDS

Sheds offer a relatively low cost option for a layout building and can be quite large, easy to assemble and easy to buy locally. However, as soon as you start looking at larger sheds, bespoke build is the only way forward and costs then sky rocket. Smaller sheds will escape the planning rules for construction warrants and permits in the UK and in other places too. But start building large structures that take up large areas of the garden and the planning authorities may take a dim view of your plans for a miniature railway empire! Smaller structures can be erected on a simple foundation of paving slabs, but anything larger than a 10ft by 8ft building really should sit on a good, solid concrete base.

The advantage of a shed is the instantly available and dedicated space with no concerns about mess resulting from construction. The concerns I had when considering a garden shed structure for my project included security, damp, the extra cost of insulation and the laying of an electrical cable from the house to the building. Such buildings can become very hot in the summer and difficult to heat in the winter. If I had to do that work, together with spending more on a bespoke shed, there had to be better options available.

OUTBUILDINGS

You may be fortunate in having a larger property with an outbuilding such as a farm steading or barn. Again, work may be needed to make such areas habitable, clean, free of damp and easy to heat in winter or keep cool in summer. Alternatively, go for a self-build log cabin which would cost little more than most large bespoke sheds and offer some very secure accommodation. Such buildings are available as kits and come in set sizes. But it may be that the available shapes do not suit your theme and the extra cost of having such a building assembled could knock it out of the frame.

The costs regarding insulation, damp-proofing and the electricity supply are broadly similar to those involved with building a shed, as are the planning issues. However, as kits, they are usually straightforward to build, very solid and well designed. A log cabin of Scandinavian design was my preferred choice for an outbuilding because it suited my budget and timescales too. I could little afford my ideal – which would have been a large block-constructed building with slate roof, one large internal room for the layout together with a toilet and kitchenette. The cabin cost £6,000, has a large internal space of nearly 360sq.ft and a high roof supported by huge purlins. It took a week to build, and little wonder, because the walls are composed of machined white cedar logs 80mm thick, the floor boards are 35mm thick and the roof timbers 25mm thick. In all, including the pre-assembled, double-glazed doors and windows, the structure weighed nearly 6 metric tons! At £16.65/sq.ft for the building and an additional £1,500 for insulation, wiring and finishing materials, I consider myself very fortunate indeed. With that financial outlay, there is the need to make the best use of the building, including its volume, hence ideas developed for a multi-deck layout to take advantage of the high roof space.

Finding a home: a bespoke 30ft building constructed by Tony Wright for his OO gauge 'Little Bytham' layout. A particular theme may require an investment to create the space needed to execute it, and long, steam-hauled East Coast main line trains in 4mm scale warranted this level of expenditure even before a single baseboard had been constructed. (PHOTO: TONY WRIGHT)

Finding a home: the start of my grand project was marked by the ground works for the cabin base, which was composed of a slab of concrete 100mm thick placed on a prepared base of aggregate, sand and a water-bar membrane.

The cabin base is seen placed on the slab and squared off. Note the gravel around the concrete slab for drainage.

Construction consists of assembling the walls of machined logs that lock together using a tongue and groove system.

While this photograph shows the main structure assembled, the detail work of such a project, such as finishing around the windows and doors, together with protective treatments, can take almost as long to complete.

Internally, another damp-proof membrane is placed under the wooden floor, together with insulation material.

PREPARING THE SPACE

Taking time to prepare the layout space is very important if the environment is to be a pleasing and comfortable place to spend time – a lot of time! Give thought to seating, stools, a small table for drinks, storage and to making the layout space as uncluttered as possible. Presentation is important so as not to detract from your lovely model. In my case, I was keen to make the cabin as uncluttered and as clean an environment as possible for guest operators, visitors and my regular operating team. Storage for equipment and materials was important, as was heating and making space for people as well as track.

Comfort and security were considered from the word go; I emphasized the importance of providing a damp-proof membrane when discussing the concrete base with the ground works contractor. The membrane

was installed before the concrete was poured. The slab was left to cure for thirty days and allowed to dry for further time so that the water used to make the concrete workable and for the hydration of the cement could escape. The frame of the building was placed on damp-proof material before the structure was erected upon it. Once the building was complete, further damp-proof material was installed under the floor boards, together with as much insulation material as I could squeeze in.

Such is the character of the building, I was reluctant to hide the beautiful timber walls and roof by insulation material. However, it was vital to insulate against heat loss in winter and solar heat gain in summer. My wife Sarah discovered a liquid insulation material based on nano technology that was applied direct to the wood with a paint roller. It reduced the heating load from 4kW of heating to a single 2kW oil-filled radiator in

Creating a comfortable atmosphere is very important, no matter the location of your railway. Insulation, heating, cooling and lighting all have their part to play. The cabin was treated with a liquid insulation product to retain heat in winter and reflect solar heat in summer.

Nansulate is the trade name for nano technology insulation that was used in my layout building. Notably, this sort of product could help with the insulation of lofts, sheds, garages and other locations where traditional insulating products would be awkward to apply.

It looks like acrylic varnish and is applied in the same way, with a roller. Painting equipment can be washed with water after application.

winter while maintaining a healthy 20°C. Consideration was given to an air-to-air heat source pump for heating and cooling, the idea being to control yet further the environment of the building and its contents. After all, there was a lot of expensive equipment in use within those walls. Consideration was also given to carpeting, a seating area for guests and off-duty operators and a music system for playing CDs during construction sessions.

The doors and windows are fitted with additional security locks, there is a CO_2 fire extinguisher in the building that is suitable for dealing with electrical fires, and the electricity supply in the cabin has its own distribution box with fuses and safety devices. The cable leading from the house to the cabin is an armoured

This is me, at work, rolling Nansulate directly on to the wooden surfaces of the cabin. (I must apologize for the awful clothes, but when in scruffy mode ...)

one and, when choosing such cable, buy the highest rated type you can afford. With regard to the electrical installation, I employed the services of a qualified electrician. All of this effort in preparing the layout space may cost additional money and further delay the start of real layout building, but pays dividends over time when the layout is up and operational.

ONCE HAVING FOUND SOME REAL ESTATE TO BUILD THE RAILWAY ...

We have located the space for our railway that satisfies everyone as far as possible. Yes, there will be some compromises with the choice, but your skills as a modeller can be used to make the best of that space. I hope that you will have considered the access issues, construction mess, heating, ventilation, a power supply and security. The available space has been measured and checked to see whether it is usable and has a chance of fulfilling our ambitions. Now is the time to develop the layout concept.

It may be that you already have an idea of what you would like to model, but without the physical boundaries of the layout space, the actual development of ideas was going no further than a wish list. Thinking back on my 'mulling-it-over' phase, it began to reach a stage where my thoughts simply went in circles and no real decisions on the layout concept had been made as I had too many themes to choose from. With eighteen months past, there was no sign of any activity in the cabin, which was beginning to look like a very expensive storage building. What I did have on the credit side of the balance sheet was a clear view of the theme of one possible project. One cannot make a start unless decisions regarding this have been made. Here is a check list of things to consider when developing the layout concept. In essence, it is a different question regarding time and space, as you will see.

THE MODELLING THEME

A modelling (or layout) theme is the overall plan of what you want to model. Most if not all modellers have a theme in mind (or more than one, as in my case), even before the search for space commences, through an interest in a particular prototype and careful research. The choice of themes from the options that may present themselves may be determined by the available space – the two are linked. For example, if a shelf measuring 10ft long and 20in wide is all that is available, any thoughts of King's Cross station in about 1957 in OO gauge are not going to develop into a realistic theme, no matter how much it is desired. However, a smaller terminus station could be accommodated by that space if a different theme were to be considered. Alternatively, if 30ft by 20ft were to present itself as an ideal environment, the small switching layout theme that may have been in mind would soon grow to a main line with long train action.

A theme is the choice of period in time, railway company, scale, gauge, date or season and geographical location. For example, with my model collecting over the years, I have a number of themes I would like to pursue. I have a liking for US-outline N scale and mountain railroading. Montana Rail Link (MRL) is also part of that theme, my having followed the fortunes of the company since it was formed in the late 1980s. Long-distance mountain railroading plays to the strengths of N scale, enabling long trains with spectacular scenery to match, and all being possible to model in a reasonable space, thanks to the relatively small size of the models. A further factor that made me consider the MRL main line is its use as a bridge route for long-distance trains operated by Burling Northern and its 1994 merger company BNSF. The mix of big six-axle traction, long trains and colour all added up to a fascinating railway scene.

I also enjoy modelling modern railway operations in the UK, having accumulated a large collection of 4mm-scale models, ready for a layout. This saw me doodle several themes on to notepaper, including Redhill on the line to Brighton as a 'bitsa' station theme. I considered the junction at the south end of the station where the Tonbridge line diverges as the main layout feature, together with the likely traffic patterns that would make operation interesting. My collection of Southern Region multiple units, together with fine models for the Class 33 offered by Heljan,

would have fitted a theme from 1989 to 2002 perfectly. As you will see, this theme was replaced by another, that better matched the shape of my space, and sits perfectly in another part of Southern Region third rail territory.

To complicate matters, I like the Black Country railways too, that network of freight and suburban lines in the Wolverhampton, Dudley and Walsall area, with Bescot Yard and the Grand Junction line through the middle of it all. I considered Walsall as a possible location, modelled in the British Rail Sectorization era from 1987 to 1994, before the privatization of Britain's rail network. The location would take advantage of the new Bachmann Class 150/1 and Class 150/2 Sprinters, together with others that have been released as hi-fidelity models in recent times, such as the Hornby Class 31, the Bachmann Class 37 and models of the first Sprinter trains introduced in 1986, the Class 150/1s. All modelled in 4mm-scale EM gauge, of course.

As if that lot were not enough, the allure of US outline HO scale models attracts me too, something midwest in the 1980s with four-axle road power, grain trains and other agricultural traffic. Bring it more up to date and ethanol traffic would fit too. The Soo Line first grabbed my attention and then that was followed by research into the I&M Rail Link (Washington Corporation Company), sadly now a 'fallen flag'. That offered the excuse to model MRL power in HO scale. Did I mention something about having cake and eating it too? The layout could have taken the concept of a freelance line with a couple of daily trains and a lot of switching. However, I am running ahead of myself here in suggesting a layout concept. Here's more detail on deciding on a theme.

PROTOTYPE OR FREELANCE?

An interesting question, and, in truth, there is no real boundary between the two. Prototype modelling has many advantages in that the practices of the full-size railways can be followed. This is particularly useful when considering the track planning stage of layout design. The full-size railways had to work through problems and operational issues and will have resolved most if not all of the wrinkles you may encounter if designing your own track layout. Research into the railway company should turn up track diagrams and other useful material, not to mention the inevitable publications such as books and magazine features. For modellers interested in modelling more up to date themes, it may be possible to lay your hands on a great deal of company material. For example, when researching my MRL theme, I made use of an official timetable and track diagram book that I was fortunate enough to obtain from official sources. Ebay frequently turns up all sorts of material, from signalling notices to timetables.

As an alternative to prototype modelling, modellers frequently turn to a technique called 'prototype freelancing' where the equipment and identity of an existing or historical company are applied to a freelance layout design or vice versa. There may be elements of the design that have prototype features, but, in essence, the design is freelance. There is nothing to stop you from having freelance locomotives with fictional but appropriate name plates operating on a prototype-base layout. The whole point about developing a layout theme is to satisfy your modelling itches.

Fully freelanced themes are also popular, but these are often harder to reconcile; to prevent a model from looking too contrived is not easy and certainly not a route I wanted to take. There are many successful ones where careful observation of the prototype has been applied to a fictional railway company with its own created history, geography, routes, customers, yards and stations. Railway history and economic and social structures have all been thought through and applied to the theme of these successful layouts. They require a lot of imagination to create and care to design to ensure the railway works well. When considering a freelance theme, keep to the rules applied to full-size railway practice generally but otherwise, have fun.

WHERE IS THE LAYOUT TO BE LOCATED GEOGRAPHICALLY?

Another interesting question because the choice of layout location can depend on a number of factors and often the preference for a particular railway company will narrow this down. Are you interested in cities and urban areas? Modelling such locations, and they vary a great deal, brings in the opportunity for many and various types of traffic and there being more than one railway company too. Industries cluster around cities and large towns and often the arrival of industry is followed by urban sprawl as workers move into the area. Grime, soot, dirt and gritty reality are all there for the modelling, as is the excuse for a wide variety of rail traffic.

Alternatively, rural areas, including remote places, still have railways that can be very busy, despite the lack of population. Bridge routes or branch lines to remote rural communities all offer great modelling opportunities. From the mountains of the Scottish Highlands, to the tamer beauty of the English Riviera, there is a wide variety of rural landscapes to choose from. Modellers of European railways find rural France intriguing, the Alps a great scenic opportunity or the flat country of the Netherlands a challenge to portray accurately, to mention just a few of the many possibilities and I have seen them all done beautifully. There is a growing interest in the railways of the former Soviet Union countries as more information becomes available, and, of course, North America has some of the greatest railway dramas to model anywhere in the world – from sinuous lines climbing over mountain passes to the long straights of the prairies.

When planning to build a layout, think about the prototype (and its geography) that truly grabs your imagination and do some research to see whether it can be worked into a layout theme. If mountain railways in Peru take your fancy, will you be able to research them and acquire enough modelling resources to satisfy your desires? Will it fit your layout space? Can you buy enough models or kits to make the project a practicable one to complete within a reasonable time period before losing interest?

WHAT ERA?

Railways span more than 100 years and, in some countries, 150th anniversaries have passed for many rail routes. Where I live in Scotland, the Highland Railway is a favourite modelling subject together with the North British and the Caledonian too. The same routes operated by those companies also saw operations under the LMS (London Midland and Southern Railway) and British Rail. The choice of era will be determined not only by a preference for a particular railway company, but the equipment it operated as well. Sometimes, this choice is limited by the available equipment that can be bought in a given scale that would expedite the modelling of the subject. Consider the availability of models when choosing an era. Highland Railway prototypes can be modelled from kits (Lochgorm Kits makes some exquisite 4mm- and 7mm-scale kits for Highland Railway locomotives), but do you have the time and skills to build and finish them?

The choice of era is also influenced by the available research material. While much steam era equipment can still be found on railway property today, making research a simpler prospect than trying to track down important data from lines long abandoned and long dismantled, as time advances, this old infrastructure is being lost or modified to accommodate modern operations. Electrification is one of those features that completely destroys most of the older infrastructure.

Transition eras are frequently rewarding choices, and by far the most popular era in the US seems to be the steam to diesel transition (the date of which varied depending on the road), because mixing colourful diesels with steam locomotives offers the best of several worlds. The same could be said for the period straddling 1992 to 1998 in the UK. The privatization of the UK's railways did not happen overnight and new equipment acquired by private operators rubbed shoulders with older BR-built equipment in various liveries for quite a few years. As you can see, the choice of era can help with developing an interesting layout theme and an exciting layout concept can grow from it.

WHICH SEASON?

Something rarely considered by modellers is selecting a season to model. Apart from the obvious impact on scenery and layout colours, seasons also affect on railway traffic patterns. The long grain trains of North American railroading reach a peak after the harvest, for obvious reasons. Railways serving seaside resorts with terminus stations may run to a reduced timetable during the winter, with none of the long-distance holiday trains, charters and those additional services intended to cope with the higher demand for travel that would make the location a busy place in the summer. Conversely, power station coal traffic may run more frequently during the colder months, while the run up to Christmas may see an increase in deep sea container traffic on intermodal trains carrying imported retail goods and food. Choosing a season to match your freight and passenger traffic must be an important part of your layout theme, as well as your need to think about the artistic challenges of recreating dry summer landscapes or deep snow drifts in the mountains.

SCALE AND GAUGE

With a home for your layout secured, the physical space available may determine your choice of scale and track gauge. O gauge presents space challenges simply because the equipment is so physically large; while N gauge (or N scale) offers opportunities to model extensive railway systems or spectacular scenery in relatively small spaces, because it occupies a fraction of the space of O gauge.

Modellers are often divided on which scale and gauge combination is the best and so often it comes down to the availability of equipment once again. In the United States and Canada, modellers are increasingly enjoying affordable off-the-shelf O gauge models with sound and exquisite detail. British modellers still have to rely on kits for the bulk of O gauge models, thus reducing its appeal, although that situation is changing. The growing popularity of S gauge and the tiny Z gauge scales in North America is also down to the availability of a growing range of off-the-shelf products.

In the UK the two scales that dominate the market and cover the majority of interests – because of excellent commercial support – are 4mm-scale models running on 16.5mm-gauge (OO gauge) track and 2mm-scale, N gauge running on 9mm-gauge track.

In Europe, North America and elsewhere in the world, 3.5mm-scale, HO gauge is the most popular, followed by N scale, which is different from the British

N scale at being modelled to 1:160 scale instead of 1:148 scale. Again, the commercial product support in these scales is vast, making them obvious choices for many modellers, especially if equipment is shared among friends' layouts.

In all, scale and gauge can be pretty confusing, especially when you consider the various fine scales and narrow gauge railways with several hybrid combinations of scale and track gauge. Do some research and visit your model shop to look at different scale models to see which best suits your pocket, modelling skills, eyesight and desires. I suspect, like it was for me, that space will be the key factor in choosing a scale and gauge as much as a personal liking for a particular range of equipment or railway company and era.

TYPE OF TRAIN

A layout theme may be determined by a preference for train type, be it freight, mail or express passenger trains and the precise mixture of both. The choice of a location and scale may be determined by this preference. If space is tight, the choice of trains to be run on the layout will be determined by the available space. This is not necessarily too limiting when you consider the action I found I could pack into my small, portable layouts using short formation electric multiple unit stock.

When developing your theme, especially if it is freelance, give careful consideration to the train type you propose to run. A model railway without a clear and definite purpose will soon become boring to operate and unconvincing.

TIME AND DISTANCE ISSUES TO CONSIDER WHEN DEVELOPING A MODELLING THEME

It is fun and exciting to dive headlong into a new project, especially when we have uncovered research material, photographs, maps and diagrams for a location and a railway company that really appeal to us. It suits the space that we have in which to build a layout and, more importantly, has grabbed us by the inspirational scruff of the neck. Sometimes, it's a field trip to

a location we have never visited before. Realizing its modelling potential sees us scribbling track plans on the back of beer mats in the pub afterwards and speculating as to how much space the designs would gobble up, what with scale, length of trains, fiddle yards and so on. Sometimes it's the release of a brand-new model that opens up modelling possibilities for us.

I have been fortunate enough to have visited Montana and to witness MRL and BNSF operations for real as a railway enthusiast. With the photography and research notes I have pulled together, I can model railroad action that is many thousands of miles removed from where I live. However, for some this sort of field work might not be possible and some purists have asked if it is right to contemplate a project theme for which the prototype inspiration has come from magazines, DVDs and published photographs alone.

This self-limiting thinking can stifle creativity and the freethinking desire to model something that really grabs us – it's something I hear from other modellers when chatting at exhibitions, and now I find myself doing the same thing. Comments about my modelling Southern Region EMUs, when I live in the north, demonstrate that people do think of the geographical location of their layout themes relative to where they live. Thinking further about it, there is a relationship of sorts between time and distance in the planning of our layouts. Think of a thirty-year-old modeller living in Frankfurt considering modelling the Baltimore & Ohio? Both distance from the geographical region and time impact on the ability to create a realistic B&O model in a modeller's basement in Frankfurt.

So, how do you reconcile modelling a prototype that is many thousands of miles away from home and be able to justify your choice of modelling theme even if you have never visited it? After reading an article in an American modelling magazine (probably *Model Railroader*), by a modeller based in the US, describing how he decided to model a prototype at the other end of the country, in a different state, which was several thousand miles away, I realized that his research challenge was little different from mine – he was a long way from his chosen location and flying would be the only practicable way to get there. In addition to that, the prototype was a 'fallen flag' railroad that had been absorbed into one of the larger companies many years earlier. He had the dual problems of distance and time period to resolve, yet did not see it as a barrier to achieving his goal, not dissimilar to the situation British modellers have when considering the modelling of overseas railways.

In many ways, the time and distance issue applies within the UK too because it's equally as challenging for a modeller living in Kent to execute the building of a layout based on the Highland Railway at the end of the nineteenth century. How about a modeller based in Scotland considering a layout based on the South Coast line in Sussex at the end of the slam door EMU era? It too raised the issues of distance and historical time to consider.

In the end, I decided that it was too much philosophical nonsense to worry about where the prototype was located and how long ago it existed. The distance issue can be resolved with planes, trains and automobiles. The time issue can be resolved by careful research in libraries, on the Internet and other such places where historical records are archived. Enthusiasts' groups and historical societies with online Special Interest Groups (SIGs) provide another way of uncovering the vital details required to build and operate a convincing layout. In many cases remnants of the old railway may still exist and a field trip could reveal a great deal of information on the ground that otherwise may not be available in a published format. Anyway, the landscape may not have changed much and photographs of the surrounding terrain are as important as images of the railway itself.

As for my grand layout scheme, I discovered that the best way to uncover those vital little details was to make friends with like-minded enthusiasts over the Internet and through societies that cater for those interests. It is interesting to note that many of those people live close to the area that I propose to model, sometimes work for the railroad company concerned and are unceasingly generous with their time and help. And that is reciprocated for the British outline modellers among them who are also tackling the same issues of time and distance, but in the opposite direction. For someone living in Seattle, a ScotRail Class 170 Turbostar is a remarkably exotic creature to model, while a Scot living in Edinburgh would find Seattle Sounder trains quite different from the second-generation diesel multiple units that operate suburban routes in the Central Belt. So, where did I file that picture of that MRL SD-45?

WHEN THE PROTOTYPE RAILWAY DOES NOT DELIVER – EXPANDING THE ENVELOPE

Some modellers like to develop freelanced layout themes for a railway and they can be as fictional as having a completely made up railway company and line as well, but modelled to exacting standards based on true prototype practice, making them as real and believable as modelling a full-size railway, past or present. Some modellers use elements of the full-size railway they are interested in and rearrange them to suit their space and desired operation. I know of modellers who extend the locomotive fleet to suit a choice of fictitious numbers and names too.

The boundaries are limitless and themes can be developed, with part freelance, part true prototype modelling to suit the modeller. For example, I extended my British outline modelling to cover sectorization to privatization, a period of fifteen years from 1989 to 2004. Yet few actual locations stay the same for so long, so, at some point, my combination of liveries and rolling stock might not be strictly correct for the manner in which the location was modelled. At this point, we enter the realm of compromise to suit the modeller, and compromise is not a bad thing if it means you have a working model that satisfies your needs.

One way of looking at such issues is either to choose a specific year and time of year to suit your scenery and model both stock and location to fit them exactly, or do what I have considered doing and go for the broad time period for stock, while restricting the layout location to a narrower period to ease the choice of features. The actual trains themselves will be modelled accurately for the period in which they ran for as long as they are appropriate to the location modelled. But in all of this, remember that your layout is your railway and you are free to develop it as you wish.

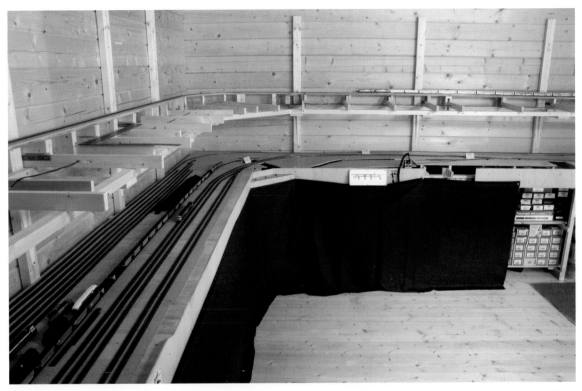

At last, some quality layout space. The layout concept may now be developed. Those tall ceilings in this building have given me an idea for my layout concept: more than one deck!

SO, WITH DECISIONS MADE –

I eventually settled on prototype modelling with two definite themes, and one undecided as to the prototype location to suit an interesting multi-deck layout. Concepts are a part of layout planning, which is covered in the next chapter. Here are my conclusions:

Montana Rail Link c.1992–98 to 1:160 N scale representing the 4th Sub Division 'water level route' in summer using elements of the route between Missoula and Paradise, Montana. The theme allows for point-to-point operation with freight trains up to 10ft in length, including block trains of grain and soya beans in covered hoppers, unit coal trains, double-stack intermodal trains and local trains of mixed train formations. Purely a freight railroad in real life, my version may see the return of a daily Amtrak service. To be built in two phases to ease cost.

Top deck layout to be a scenic test track to EM gauge using Folkestone East as a 'layout design element'. A circular layout to be built in two phases, starting with the main lines and fiddle yards. This is to provide a home for my extensive collection of third rail Southern Region slam-door EMUs and freight stock appropriate to the area. Locomotives to include Class 33s, Class 47s and Class 73s. Phase 2 will incorporate the yard and berthing sidings. A representation of the Folkestone Harbour branch will form phase 3, offering the excuse to run charter trains.

A North American HO scale theme in late summer or early autumn set in the Mid West, representing agricultural freight traffic. The old east–west Milwaukee Road through Mason City, Iowa, which became the I&M Rail Link and latterly the Chicago, Iowa & Eastern is a possibility. Anyone knowing that location may also know something unique and electric about the railroads of that particular city...

CHAPTER TWO

LAYOUT CONCEPTS

Tall ceilings led me to consider a multi-deck concept. The lower two decks are linked by a helix and host the Montana Rail Link N scale theme, while the upper deck (shown here with slam door multiple units helping with the track plan) was intended for a circular scenic test track, which has swiftly developed into a full-blown theme based on a prototype location on the Kent coast main line, together with room for another theme on the opposite side of the supports seen in this picture. Three decks, three different layout themes.

THE LAYOUT CONCEPT

With your theme clearly in mind and the outline plan written down in a project book, you can look to applying it to an appropriate layout concept. This is, in effect, the overall or 'top-level' plan of what you are going to fit into your available space and what type of layout is to be constructed to suit the layout theme. You are still not at the track planning or detailed layout design stage just yet, but looking at more general ideas and considerations for the model.

One technique introduced to US outline modellers by the late and much missed John Armstrong, a modeller highly respected among model railroaders in North America for his skills in layout planning and design, is the concept of 'Givens and Druthers'. I use this useful planning tool in the development of my own layouts with much success. The idea is that there are fixed parameters that will be difficult to change when working on both the layout concept and when getting down to the detailed planning, these he called

'Givens'. We are probably painfully aware of what those things are in our particular case. On the opposite side of the coin are the 'Druthers', those features we would much like to see in the concept and plan for the layout. A wish-list if you like, something concrete to take to the detailed planning stage.

This is my list of Givens and Druthers for the layout concept to accommodate my three layout themes. It may surprise you.

GIVENS

- Layout to be accommodated in an outbuilding remote from the house.
- No construction work or materials to be left anywhere in the living areas of the home.
- Available space is limited to 18ft by 18ft over external dimensions, as determined by the largest outbuilding that can be erected in Scotland without the need for planning consent and building warrants (assuming that no more than 50 per cent of the garden

A single-deck 'round the walls' layout concept using modular box frame baseboards constructed of plywood is the foundation for Tony Wright's 'Little Bytham'. For convenience, the baseboard frames of plywood box construction were manufactured to a high standard by a professional joiner off-site and delivered in modules ready for assembly. (PHOTO: TONY WRIGHT)

is taken up; distance from boundary lines and distance from the main dwelling house also comply with the rules; regulations in your area may vary, so please check).

- The cabin has to accommodate a photo-stage and modelling work bench in addition to the layout, so not all of the floor area can be given over to a layout.
- An area has to be set aside for a small operating crew area with seating, which can also be used by family members spending time with me when I am in the mood for modelling.
- The layout has to be presented neatly with no clutter or exposed timber when complete.
- Storage needs have to be allowed for in the design of the layout.

- No low, duck-under access to the middle of the layout, ruling out the traditional oval design for the lower decks.
- The layout is to be operated using Digital Command Control equipment.

DRUTHERS

- A multi-deck design is envisaged to enable the building of three of my layout themes.
- Two decks to be used to accommodate the MRL N scale theme to 1:160 scale, with a long main line run.
- The top deck to accommodate the British outline Southern Region theme to 4mm-scale, EM gauge c.1989–2004.
- A second small HO scale North American switching layout to be accommodated on the

top deck separated from the British layout by a scenic back drop.

- A helix to be used to connect the first two decks to achieve the long main line run required for the MRL N scale theme.
- Wireless throttles to be introduced when funds allow and used whenever possible to permit roaming control and easy control of the upper deck layout as the technology becomes available in the UK.
- Speed of construction to be assisted by North American layout construction techniques, such as L-girder construction.
- No cabinet-grade joinery necessary. Everything will be hidden by scenery in due course.
- Construction time: five years with the first fourteen months to build the skeleton from floor to running trains, as described in this book.

It could be that the various options for a layout concept may not have been suggested to you before, and, without that, building up a list of 'Druthers' may not be as simple a task as you thought. Here are some ideas of the different concepts you could use: think about the layout size, whether it is to be portable or fixed and the cost of construction too. How will it be maintained and how much time is available to you to actually build it so that it can be operated, never mind finished, with structures and scenery?

WHAT TYPE OF LAYOUT CONCEPT?

The layout concept will be determined partly by your theme and partly by the space you have available to you. Other factors are whether you are likely to move in the foreseeable future or whether the chosen location for the layout will be available for only part of the time. You may go for a fixed layout concept, which is easier to build and wire up, because you do not have to factor in things such as baseboards joints, storage racks and a foolproof way of setting the layout up precisely enough so that the tracks line up correctly time after time.

A large, oval-shaped layout is a commonly chosen concept, with a scenic model at one side and fiddle yard

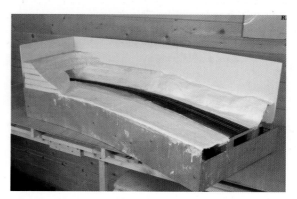

The smallest layouts one could consider are dioramas such as this one built to test scenic techniques or 'micro-layouts'.

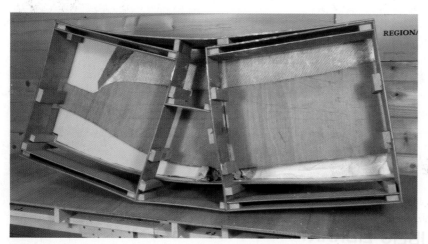

The construction of the diorama board was very simple and was built from material left over from past projects.

One advantage of portable layouts, such as Platform 4a and 4b, is being able to take them to train shows and exhibitions for display. This shows the layout on display at a Falkirk show in 2005 and the fiddle yard to terminus (or end-to-end) concept is clearly demonstrated, a popular one for small layouts. Yet, despite a simple track plan and small size, it packs a lot of action and visual interest.

Another view of Platform 4a and 4b, a layout concept based on modelling part of a larger station. The main through lines are represented on the right and are seen occupied by a postal train, which are a static part of the layout.

or staging yard to the rear. This is a very traditional approach. Small spaces call for the shunting plank, while long, narrow spaces may suit a shelf layout. The luxury of a large basement calls for all manner of convoluted designs with peninsulas and around-the-walls schemes. They may also be called 'walk-in' designs because the aisles between the baseboards are accessible, often allowing the trains to be followed by the operator as they run over the main line.

There is cross-over between the various designs too. A round-the-walls scheme may also be described as a linear design, with a main line that runs from east to west or A to B, depending on how you view it. There will be some link incorporated into the track plan to allow continuous running for display purposes too. You can have a walk-in, linear layout that is a multi-deck too. My MRL N scale theme has turned out to be a linear design with a walk-in central area for access to all of the east–west main line. The layout proposed for the top deck is a loop layout or continuous run with fiddle yard to the rear for staging trains between runs. Here are some more ideas for a layout concept.

LEFT: 'Courcelle – Part' is a beautiful O gauge layout based on French operations built by Richard Chown and is seen here when out on the exhibition circuit. It is operated as an end-to-end layout with a small sector plate fiddle yard just visible behind the train. Scenically, it represents part of a larger station scene, a modelling concept that offers much potential for the space-starved modeller.

Arran Aird's 'Morven Terminal' is based on modern US operations with intermodal trains dominating the scene. The layout is portable, frequently displayed at train shows and is modelled to N scale with a continuous loop run. The scenic area is to the front and the staging yard to the rear. A control panel is located at the end of the layout and there is no central operating well.

SINGLE DECK

The track is constructed on a single deck with inclines and gradients but no second level. There may or may not be a second level to the layout, that is, where a line crosses another on a bridge. They are by far the simplest layouts to build but restrict the true real estate area to a single baseboard level.

MULTI-LEVEL

A multi-level layout has tracks on more than one level, but within the same scenic area. This enables the modeller to introduce more track to the layout without its appearing crowded, and the use of different levels adds scenic and visual interest. Bridges and other civil engineering features can be modelled, but be careful not to have a high-level line with no apparent reason for it to exist.

TWIN DECK

A twin-deck layout has two clearly separated decks which are not scenically connected to each other. The tracks on the second deck are further along the line from those on the lower deck. Twin-deck layouts are used to great advantage to extend the length of a main line, increase the distance between towns and to make yards and passing sidings longer for longer trains. At the cost of the greater complexity of the joinery and the higher construction costs over a single deck, you get up to twice the railway for a given space. Remember, you will need a physical connection between the two unless you plan to execute a completely different theme on the second deck – a great way of having two different layout themes in one space.

MULTI-DECK

Three or more decks are possible, assuming that you have the head room to accommodate them, the joinery skills to build them and enough time to fill them. The issues with multi-deck layouts are the same as those with twin-deck layouts in terms of cost and complexity of construction, but with one added problem: access to the top deck may need steps and that adds complexity to construction and operations, especially if any of your layout operators are height-challenged.

MUSHROOM DESIGN

An interesting concept is to model a layout which rises over its length to gain altitude, either to represent a line operating through and over mountain territory or as a way to physically link separate decks located one over another. The floor is built up to match the gradient of the line for operator comfort so that the trains can be easily followed. The problem with this type of design is the additional cost of building up part of the floor and the design has to allow for ceiling height in the railway room. As a layout rises towards the ceiling, layout lighting may become more challenging to install without becoming a problem for the operators.

END-TO-END

End-to-end layouts are popular in the UK because they can be built as shelf layouts or portables. They usually consist of a scenic section either at one end or in the middle with a fiddle yard at the opposite end to the scenic section or at both ends. The concept is one of a theatrical set up with the fiddle yards as the wings and the scenic section as the stage for the players, which in our case are the model trains themselves. While end-to end layouts are usually simple to build, they offer fairly restricted train lengths and relatively limited operations. Some 'micro-layout' designs are based on small end-to-end designs, where a fiddle yard traversing table or sector plate forms part of the run round for a freight yard or station, a visual trick to give the illusion of greater space. They have the advantage in being feasible to construct in a small space and not too costly to finish, either in time or money.

PORTABLE

Portable layouts are built as modules that bolt precisely together, either free-standing or for placing on a table top for convenience. The design must allow for the precise alignment of each board, a convenient size of module for carrying and storage, and a light-weight design of baseboard that is easy to lift. Some portable layouts may reach a very large size and the choice of scale and gauge has not deterred the building of some monster projects in O gauge and even Gauge 1! Almost any layout concept can be built to be portable, including multi-level, end-to-end and oval-shaped.

A multi-level layout is shown under construction, with a yard scene on the lower level and the main line crossing it on what will become a series of bridges. The model is a linear design with a fiddle yard at one end and provision to make it an end-to-end layout with two off-stage areas if required. It is 12ft in length, built to be portable and modelled to British 4mm-scale, EM gauge. Called 'Dudley Heath Yard', it is, at the time of writing (2009), my current portable layout project intended for display at train shows.

The Inverness and District Model Railway Club owns a large, multi-level N scale exhibition layout that consists of a series of ovals and a large staging yard hidden behind the mountainside. A helix is used to connect the two levels to each other and provides visual interest when the layout is exhibited at train shows.

An example of a multi-level layout is this fully operational project built by Graeme Elgar. It is a good example of a home layout constructed to be free-standing with modular boards, so that it may be dismantled and moved if required. Called 'Cold Blow Lane', the theme is BR Southern Region, with the Bricklayers' Arms yard as the central layout design element used for inspiration. While based on a prototype and with prototype operations, it is a fictitious model.

'Cold Blow Lane' again showing the elevated main line and tracks running down grade to the yard. Using two levels like this increases the visual interest of a layout and is a useful design concept to obtain more railway for a given area without using the twin or multi-deck concept.

The main line crosses the yard access on Graeme's layout, with the yard visible beyond.

Another view of my portable layout, Platform 4a and 4b. The theme for this could be summarized thus: South West Trains (Stagecoach) and Thames Trains together with related companies c.1998–2004, located in Berkshire and modelled in 4mm-scale, EM gauge. To be operated with EMU and other related Southern Region slam door stock and Class 165 and Class 166 Turbo units. The view here shows a Class 207 DEMU, a Class of suburban unit once closely related to train operations between Reading and Basingstoke. Pushing the envelope of the theme a little means that I can include them in an era where they had long been displaced by more modern stock. You can do that too if you wish; it's your model after all.

BELOW: The East Neuk Model Railway Club built a large, portable N gauge layout based on modern practice on the West Coast main line south of Motherwell. This view shows a Class 66 operating a cement train that would have originated from Oxwellmains cement works near Dunbar. The layout is a superb piece of prototype modelling using a portable concept.

A portable layout can be designed to fit a rack or have a rack purpose-made for it to ease transportation to train shows and for storage. This layout slides neatly under one of the baseboards of the new layout.

*BELOW: **Door layouts offer opportunities to model something interesting quickly in a limited space. Doors can be purchased for relatively little from home improvement stores and make great baseboard tops when building a layout. The final layout plan was drawn out on lining paper and set track by Kato called Unitrack was used, making construction very simple indeed.***

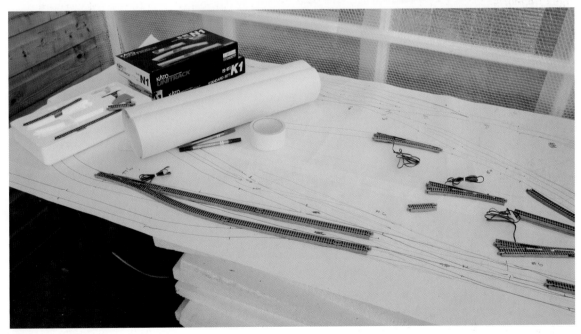

DOOR LAYOUT

A popular concept for newcomers to the hobby to try as a first layout is to construct a layout on a door because it is quick, simple and cheap. Some experienced builders have been known to build large projects on doors, using them as modules or dominoes instead of constructing separate baseboards from scratch. The doors themselves can be fitted with folding legs to make the layout free-standing and portable too.

Another view of the 'layout on a door' concept with a scenic divider built at an angle across the layout to separate the two different scenes located on opposite sides of the layout to disguise the oval track plan.

The scenic base of the 'layout on a door' was constructed from foam board and built up against the scenic divider to create steep hillsides. The Kato Unitrack looks the part on this N scale project.

HOW BIG SHOULD
THE LAYOUT BE?

Big is beautiful, as the saying goes. But is the 'biggest' or 'largest' or whatever an ideal for a model railway? Squeezing the most track, baseboards and trains into your given space without compromising the aesthetic appearance of the layout, together with grabbing as much real estate as one can, is often the main objective at this early stage. There is nothing wrong with that, and space is critical if long trains and multi-train running is part of your concept.

There is a note of caution I would like to throw into the concept-planning stage and that is this: having 1,000sq.ft or even my 360sq.ft to play with is great, but how much time can you realistically devote to construction before you have an operating railway? Not necessarily a scenic railway, but one with track, running trains and complete control systems in place? If you can only spare an hour or two a week due to family commitments or work load, trying to fill even my 360sq.ft with a single deck is going to be a struggle unless you are prepared to plan for construction over a very long period. There is always the risk that interest will be lost and new themes may present themselves, further diluting your effort.

On the other hand, spreading a large project over a longer time span also lessens the impact on the construction cost. I calculate that I shall spend between £70 to £85/sq.ft of baseboard on my project by the time it is finished. That includes the timber, tools, fixings, track, scenery, structures and the control system. It may seem like a lot of cash. However, one board has a 3ft long trestle on the N Scale MRL main line for which the base kits enabling me to build it cost over £50 alone.

The smaller the layout, the higher the cost actually becomes because the purchase price of decent control equipment may be about the same, regardless of how big the layout turns out to be. Factor in the time and cost elements of the layout and budget carefully. The initial outlay is always high as the purchases of wood, fixings, track and wiring are usually made at the start. As trains start to run and the scenery stage becomes closer, the rate of outlay falls, because scenery materials are generally lower in price for a given area of

coverage and detailing a layout takes more time than building baseboards.

So, assuming that you can cover the cost and have sufficient time to build the design; have you given consideration to on-going maintenance? Building the 1,000sq.ft plus monster brings a great deal of track to clean, wiring to check and rolling stock to maintain. How many locomotives are required to operate layouts of that size? Assuming that you can afford to buy them, they all need their wheels cleaned and gears lubricated; Digital Command Control (DCC) users will have to find funds for decoders too, in most cases.

In terms of cleaning wheels on locomotives and rolling stock, here is an illustration of how time consuming maintaining a fully operational large layout could prove to be. The MRL N scale theme has been worked into a long, single-track main line run in hill country. It is a linear concept with end-to-end operations, allowing for the modelling of selectively compressed long freight trains, roughly a third to a quarter of the length of the full-size trains. That still means twenty-five-car grain trains with three locomotives up front. Those trains are 10ft in length, making the loop length and staging track requirement longer than that.

Consider this: a thirty-car train of bogie freight cars has 120 axles or 240 wheels to clean, also check the back-to-back gauge measurements for reliable running. My layout will need a total of 350 cars plus passenger cars: a total of 1,400 axles and 2,800 wheels. Not to mention two couplers per freight car that may need periodic checks and repairs. The main line run will be over 200ft long, plus there is 100ft of track in the helix – that is over 600ft of rail *excluding* passing sidings, spurs and the yard roads – all of which will also need to be kept clean. That is definitely an important consideration when looking at layout size. So it is worth thinking twice about the size of the layout that both you and a group of friends may be able to handle before filling every inch with track and trains. It may be that your theme may fit a smaller plan, yet still deliver all of the objectives you wished to achieve and with a more manageable layout.

With the theme decided upon, space found for the layout and a layout concept in mind, it is time to move on to detailed layout design. How are you going to fill your treasured real estate efficiently?

CHAPTER THREE

DETAILED LAYOUT DESIGN

The rolling stock for the layout should be used to determine train lengths and their impact on the track plan. It may seem strange that the track plan is being devised after the baseboards have been built. However, no matter how much planning you do before construction, the track plan will be constrained by the space you have to work with, whereas careful layout planning may help you to get a better layout in your given space.

INTRODUCTION

When modellers talk about layout planning, especially in detail, they immediately reach for a pad and pencil to sketch track plans. For me, track plans are just part of the story, a small part in fact. I am more interested in 'layout design' that incorporates a variety of different considerations, which will make the building and operation of the layout more enjoyable. Layout design determines how the layout will fill the space, its impact on the room and be human-friendly too; how will the operators actually be able to put the layout into use as you intended?

Consider then, the following: aisle width, baseboard height, baseboard width, duck-under access, access to central aisles and operating wells, layout deck separation, carpet colour … yes, they are all things to plan for, even down to the colour of the fascia and where the programming or service track for DCC layouts is best located.

This chapter looks at the things you should consider when designing your layout: track layout planning and layout design. I focus more on the latter when planning layouts because it is how the layout is incorporated

into the space that affects how we relate to it. A shabby design with no comforts and awkward control won't have your operating crew returning in a hurry, no matter how good the track plan was on paper and how much real ale you have to hand. Once again, John Armstrong's invaluable planning method, 'Givens and Druthers', had a role to play in formulating my final plans before I started work.

Interestingly enough, as I looked at information from the full-size railways I was intending to model to incorporate them into a detailed design, I quickly realized that the Montana Rail Link 4th Subdivision would provide the ideal layout theme out of all of the main line locations I could have chosen from that railroad. I did consider the fascinating operations on the 3rd Subdivision over the Continental Divide at Mullan Pass, but that is already a popular modelling subject. Instead, I went for the curving lines, rock cuttings and trestles of the 4th Subdivision along the Clark Fork River. Examination of my research material and the MRL 'System Profile Book' indicated that a model of a selectively compressed segment of the route would fit my space beautifully: main line running with long trains through scenery with minimal shunting plays to the strengths of N scale modelling. While at this detailed planning and design stage, I had to reconcile myself to the realization that the top-deck British theme modelled to 4mm scale based on the junction south of Redhill would not fit without unacceptable levels of compromise – even though this was to be a scenic test track of some description. Hence, after a thorough search through Quail Maps for a suitable location, it was decided to change it to Folkestone East, even though this would restrict the passenger stock to one division of the former Southern Region of British Rail.

Before deciding on track plans, here is a more detailed list of the druthers for the two layout themes which directly affect the layout design:

THE 4TH SUBDIVISION (WATER LEVEL ROUTE) OF MONTANA RAIL LINK (FORMERLY THE NORTHERN PACIFIC MAIN LINE) THROUGH SOUTH-WEST MONTANA

- To be modelled in US-outline N scale, 1:160 scale on 9mm gauge track.
- Atlas code 55 fine N scale track to be used throughout, with some space-saving curved turnouts hand-built using the products from the Canadian track kit company called Fast Tracks.
- To occupy the bottom and the middle deck of the layout, linked by a helix to create a long east to west linear main line run of at least 220 linear feet.
- The modelled section of the line to start at the west reception and departure roads at West Missoula at milepost 123, and include the short double track section to DesMet Junction at milepost 126 where the 10th Sub diverges from the 4th Sub.
- To model the water level 4th Sub route along the Clark Fork River.
- The line is to be modelled as a single track line with passing places, west to Paradise Mont; at milepost 219 there is another yard and the 10th Sub rejoins the main line.
- The line to be 'sincere', where no trains pass through the same scene twice in an operating session or even on a single run.

- The line to be viewed facing south, with east-bound trains running right to left and west-bound trains running left to right, no matter which part of the scenic layout is viewed.
- Hidden track (off-stage) sections to be kept to a minimum; those lines forming off-stage sections of line to be accessible either by removable back scenes or by being partially concealed by scenic features.
- Off-stage loops to be incorporated so that trains can be restaged easily after operating sessions without having to traverse the whole length of the main line again.
- Minimal non-railroad structures to be modelled (modelling buildings is not my forte).
- As much railroad infrastructure from the route to be included as 'Layout Design Elements', including Bridge 165 at 'Fish Creek', which is a large steel trestle, and some of the tunnels on that section of the route.
- As much hill country scenery to be incorporated as possible: rocks, trees and, of course, a representation of the Clark Fork River itself.
- Passing sidings long enough to accommodate freight trains up to thirty cars in length.
- The minimum of storage roads as some trains can be staged mid-run on the layout and in the helix too.
- Turnouts in yards and to access industrial spurs to be manually controlled.
- Minimum turnout size to be No. 7 (1:7) on the main line and No. 5 (1:5) in off-stage areas such as staging yards.
- Minimum plain running line track radius to be 16in as determined by tests with my longest wheelbase rolling stock.
- Main line turnouts to be powered by Circuitron 'Tortoise' turnout motors and stationary DCC decoders.
- To be constructed in two phases: lower deck with continuous run together with the helix and extension of the lower deck main line over the peninsula; the main line on the second deck together with the western end staging yard to form the second phase.

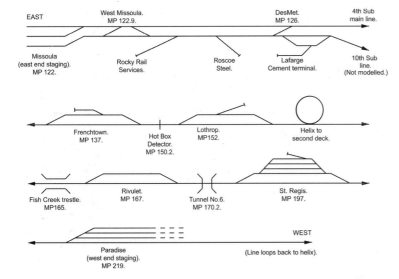

FIG. 1: The initial choice of Layout Design Elements along the MRL 4th Subdivision line was decided upon after studying photographs taken during field trips and after examining the MRL Track Profile Book. This diagram shows the first line diagram of how the layout would look.

FOLKESTONE EAST (ALSO KNOWN AS FOLKESTONE JUNCTION) KENT COAST MAIN LINE SCHEME

- To be modelled to 4mm scale, EM gauge.
- Track on the scenic section to follow prototype practice using code 82 flat bottom rail on main running lines and code 75 bull head rail in sidings.
- Off-stage areas to be laid using off-the-shelf C&L Finescale flexi track regardless of rail type.
- Double-track circular design allowing for continuous running as a scenic test track for my model building.
- Two fiddle or staging yards to be incorporated in the design, one representing Dover and the other Ashford so end-to-end operation can be staged, keeping the layout 'sincere' if required.
- Fiddle yards to be stub ended and long enough to accommodate ten-coach trains.
- Constructed as a shelf layout on the third level of the layout concept with operation from the viewing side only, although step boxes to allow operation of the layout to be high enough to see over the back scene so that the fiddle yards may be monitored too.
- Simple turnout controls using rotary switches for the fiddle yard tracks.
- Modern track to be modelled together with the conductor rail (non-energized).

- To incorporate recognizable layout design elements, including Martello Tunnel and the distinctive 1950s Kent Coast Folkestone East signal box.
- Simple track layouts required in the plan for reliability.
- Hand-built turnouts using copper-clad sleepers in the staging yards to keep costs under control.
- Laser-cut timber turnouts with hand-laid track for the scenic part of the layout.
- Minimum plain running line track radius to be 36in, as determined by tests with my longest wheelbase rolling stock and the close coupling of multiple-unit stock models.
- To be constructed in three phases, phase 2 being the yard scene and phase 3 the harbour branch line.
- To be operated with DCC equipment and (eventually) radio throttles.

INTRODUCING THE 'LAYOUT DESIGN ELEMENT' (LDE)

One hugely valuable planning technique I have adopted is the 'layout design element' (LDE), a planning and design technique now routinely used by modellers in North America, which I believe most modellers have been practising by default for many years. This technique

Folkestone East signal box: a layout design element within a larger one. It is a signature structure of the location too, as is the adjacent Martello Tunnel and the Martello Tower on the hillside above. All these features should place the layout in context. (PHOTO: AUTHOR'S COLLECTION, PHOTOGRAPHER AND DATE UNKNOWN)

BELOW RIGHT: A view from the level crossing on the Folkestone harbour branch after closure. This will form Phase 2 of the Folkestone themed layout. As an LDE, it has much to offer, including a harbour scene with small boats, a swing bridge (disused) and an interesting but short stretch of line running close to the town's buildings.

was introduced by the modeller and magazine editor Tony Koester, who has long been a contributor to *Model Railroader* magazine. He sees layout planning involving prototype information as the use of distinct scenic elements linked by neutral areas. Called LDEs, it involves the use of clearly recognized railway features from the past or present to build up a convincing layout design. An LDE could be an entire station or freight yard that would comprise the entirety of the layout design, or it could be a single structure, such as a signal box, bridge or freight depot. I personally regard the trains as LDEs too, as the length and type of train directly influence the design of any layout.

I chose several layout design elements to build up my plans. On the MRL scheme, LDEs include the distinctive junction and cement terminal as DesMet Junction (milepost 126). Also included is the passing loop (siding) at Frenchtown, Montana (milepost 137), the hot box detector at Lothrop, Montana (milepost 150.2) and the small yard at St Regis, Montana (milepost 197).

Folkestone East is one of those locations that could be considered a complete LDE in itself, occupying the whole on-stage part of the layout. The scene includes the distinctive signal box Martello Tunnel, the electrified railway itself, two very short staff halt platforms, which are staggered from each other, and the train roads for the turn-back on to the Folkestone Harbour branch.

Folkestone Harbour, once again showing the modelling potential of this location.

Trains are a form of LDE too; they are also a signature element of a location and the length of them also has a significant impact on the track plan and overall layout design, not to mention the operating plan. Do not leave the trains out of your planning calculations.

ABOVE: **This signal bridge is located on the MRL 4th Sub at DesMet Junction. It is a notable LDE for the location and is to be included on my model.**

ABOVE RIGHT: **BNSF 8241 approaches DesMet Junction with a west-bound coal drag. The signals are important in controlling the junction and access to the single line 4th Sub (CTC signalling) and the single track 10th Sub that diverges at this location and is controlled by using Track Warrants.**

Inspiration for my MRL layout came from locations like this one, with BNSF 4978 leading a mixed train of auto racks and double stack boxes up the west side of Mullan Pass on the MRL 3rd Sub, with a service for Denver. You cannot have everything on a layout, not even with selective compression, so this scene is not included in my plan. However, the train itself is likely to be!

ABOVE: *Frenchtown, Montana (milepost 137) on the 4th Sub, with its passing siding, is an LDE I am including in my plan. That cluster of buildings is an interesting feature. Note the target signals, powered turnout switch and the gentleman taking a keen interest in my observations. He had no need to worry, I had permission to be there. The town is also quite an interesting location to model.*

LEFT: *Lothrop, Montana is an LDE I have chosen to include in my 4th Sub MRL N scale plan because of the location of a nearby hot box detector and the inclusion of a cripple and maintenance of way siding off the loop. The Clark Fork River is just behind the line at this point, and the view has been taken facing west.*

RIGHT: *The scenery along the water-level route of MRL's 4th Sub is beautiful. The rounded hills will make a perfect backdrop to the hill country part of the layout, which will be located on the second deck of the layout.*

BELOW: *Simple features such as this ungated railroad crossing at milepost 154 will make interesting scenes to model, emphasize the remoteness of the country and be a reason for operators to sound their horns to warn motorists of their approach. The Clark Fork River can be seen in the background. There is a mass of detail to see in this picture: note the colour of the ballast, the use of wooden ties (sleepers), cross bucks and the milepost sign. For the back scene, the shape of the distant hills, together with rock cuttings provide valuable inspiration.*

Modellers in the UK use a term that is also useful in layout design. You may hear reference to 'signature' scenes, and these are loosely the same thing: features that clearly place a layout within its time and space, including all the elements that may affect the design of a layout. These could include the choice of trains, figures, scenery and items such as motor vehicles. Tony Koester's LDEs are more specific with regard to layout design though, and the concept is used as a specific layout design tool.

*RIGHT: **One of the most ambitious layout design elements to be included on the layout is Fish Creek trestle at milepost 165. This can be modelled by using parts from Micro Engineering trestle kits, which are available in both HO and N scale.***

*BELOW: **It is the wonderful mix of colours and liveries seen on MRL's main line that has attracted me to this particular location. This locale is Missoula, home of a large yard and the eastern starting point for my layout. It is also the headquarters for the Montana Rail Link together with its despatch control centre.***

TRACK PLANNING

USING TECHNOLOGY FOR TRACK PLANNING

Track planning software is increasingly popular and the programs vary in sophistication from track-layout planning to full-size, three-dimensional illustrations. Designs can be rendered in three-dimensional views to a high degree of sophistication in many programs. Another method some modellers have chosen to follow is to build up their plans in a train simulator package, using the trains they intend to model and operate. This allows for the operating of the layout in virtual space, and, it may be hoped, locating faults with the design before the first piece of timber is cut for a baseboard. Such planning will save time and money by avoiding mistakes.

There is no doubt that the use of such software has resulted in many successful layouts. I had a go at one application before realizing several important points about track planning. This is why I gave up on it and chose paper planning instead.

The space you have is a given; no amount of planning in a specialized program is going to change that.

There is no substitute for digging out the track templates and rolling stock to see visually what will fit and what does not; visualization is a very important part of layout planning, so, even if the track fits, the scene may not look right.

Software programs can hold only so much data on rolling stock and track; they cannot account for the bespoke modifications you have made to your collection or the kits you have built.

Passing your electronic plans around to friends for comment can be done by email, assuming that they have the correct software to view them; however, paper plans can be copied, scribbled on and viewed easily by anyone at any time and do not require a lap top.

I have discovered that no matter how many plans you sketch, there will always be a change to be made during construction as a new piece of information comes to light or a wrinkle in the design becomes apparent; don't stick rigidly to your designs so that the layout becomes unworkable, this is often the risk when computer plans are relied upon.

Finally, another realization struck me as I sketched out plans on the computer: I spend a lot of my time working with a personal computer on a daily basis, and to find hobby time being spent in front of the same machine seemed to be a little strange. Computers are not a hobby in my life. It was time to uninstall the software and dig out the paper track templates. Both the layout themes featured here were designed on paper and planned by using paper templates.

My personal preferences do not necessarily mean that software won't be suitable for your planning efforts. Before buying a bespoke application, try one of the free to download programs, such as that offered by Atlas. Even if the track system is not to your personal taste, it offers the chance to see whether it is likely to be helpful to you.

DOING IT ON PAPER

My preferred method is to plan on paper. Much of the detailed track planning was done after the baseboards were constructed because the size and shape of the boards was defined by my available space and therefore by what could be fitted in. In reality, most modellers work in this manner: find the space and devise the theme, choose a concept and calculate the baseboard space and design before seeing what will fit.

Doodling sketches using the scaled squares on graph paper is an enjoyable way for me to spend a few hours and it is easy to pass those sketches around. I recall passing an agreeable hour at a café in Aviemore in late May 2008 with my friend Graeme Elgar, discussing a wrinkle in my MRL plan. We were chasing a charter train from Aviemore to Kyle of Lochalsh with two Class 37s on the point at the time and a pause in the full-size railway action enabled us to grab a coffee, sitting outdoors in the warm Highland sunshine chatting through layout themes and plans. We had no laptop or software program to hand, but I did have half a dozen sheets of graph paper with my doodles on them tucked away in my camera bag and a resolution to the design problem was soon found.

When doodling on graph paper, remember how long turnouts and diamond crossings are and be sure to have calculated the radius of the minimum curve for your layout concept. In all of this, remember that the locomotives and stock you plan to run have a vote too. No matter how good your plan is, try some tests on different radii track. It's worth buying some set track of known radius to test your stock and to check clearances. Some of the photographs in this chapter demonstrate how I undertook this vital part of track and layout planning. The results may determine the design of your baseboards, how wide they should be and even whether your theme will fit.

Another idea is to obtain paper templates for your chosen turnouts, it is surprising how long a No. 6 turnout truly is. Buy a roll of wall lining paper from a home improvement store, measure out your baseboards on it using coloured pens and lay the templates out on it in the required configurations. Choose some rolling stock to determine how the length of locomotives and multiple units will fit platforms and sidings. Calculate the length of passenger and freight trains, and apply those data to the paper plan. Trace out train movements manually and sketch in the position of LDEs. This sort of visual planning soon reveals whether your turnouts will fit and whether you are making shunting necks long enough for locomotives, whether station bays are of sufficient size for multiple unit trains and run round roads adequate for the trains you wish to reverse. Look at how the layout will be operated. By doing this, I quickly changed the design of the staging yard on the Folkestone East layout from a conventional, double-ended affair to two separate yards, stub ended and located them on either side of the main running lines. Each was designated as an off-stage destination: 'Dover' and 'Ashford'.

Once the paper plan is determined, even at that scale, it can be transferred to the baseboard tops quite easily. The large paper layout with templates can be transferred by using map pins to trace the track centre lines on to the wood. Follow up with a black marker pen and transfer the templates at the same time.

ACCEPTING YOUR GIVENS WHEN TRACK PLANNING

This is difficult to do, I know, and it has taken me many years to reconcile the problem of modelling linear railways within square or rectangular rooms. Unfortunately, the shape of typical model railway space forces us to use curves, usually much sharper than the prototype, to get the much desired themes to fit our hard-won layout space. For example, the line through Folkestone East is as straight as the 'Golden Arrow' that once ran on the route, there's nothing I can do to change that. However, to fit the model in my space, each end has to have a 36in radius curve in the main line. That gobbles up over 7 of the 18ft of running length, which means that I have to place some LDEs on a curve at the Ashford end. Fortunately, the classic scenic break consisting of a tunnel exists at Folkestone East; Martello Tunnel saves my blushes at the Dover end at least. The curve is hidden in the tunnel and the portal is only partly visible, making it impossible to see through the tunnel at the non-prototypical curve from normal viewing angles. The full-size tunnel is dead straight and, when in the cab of a train, you can see straight through to the other end. Another compromise was to extend the turn back roads beyond the tunnel portal by a couple of feet to ensure that I could achieve the required length of turn back train roads and berthing sidings. It is not strictly correct, but it helps to make better use of the space and achieves my ten-coach train capacity goals.

Another compression I had to consider was the junction where the harbour branch leaves the three turn back train roads. The 1950s track layout was never going to fit my space without most of the scenic part being composed of complex track work. Remembering the function of this theme to act as a scenic test track, this would not fulfil my objectives, although with an extra foot or two, enthusiastic track builders would drool over such formations.

I looked at the simplified track layout at Folkestone East as it was pre-1999 re-signalling (see Fig. 3) to find a simpler but equally interesting track formation. Still, a couple of slips still existed that did not fit my criteria for a maintenance-easy layout. The post-1999 re-signalling layout is, on the other hand, too simple for interesting operations. That layout is shown in Fig. 2. In the end, I compromised by creating a selectively compressed plan incorporating the best bits of the pre-1999 track layout so that operation would be more interesting but without too much complexity. The result is shown in Fig. 4, including a 1:6 diamond crossing, access from two train roads to the branch line and a locomotive-holding spur for reversing train movements. Most importantly, the track formation fits the space with the use of 1:6 turnouts.

Curves and selective compression are the inevitable givens we have to incorporate into the layout design from time to time if it is going to work. Modellers are very good at visually seeing a few feet of model track as several miles of railway and curves on the layout as straight plain track. To shoehorn my MRL 4th Sub main

line into the room shape, the track curves around the peninsula and at the corners of the room. Making the track curve through scenes and creating scenic breaks dramatically lessens the effect of turn back curves on what is principally a linear route, albeit highly curved in places. However, not once does it curve back on itself, making my planning job all the more challenging and interesting.

The distances between passing sidings and towns on the real MRL are quite large. However, I have only

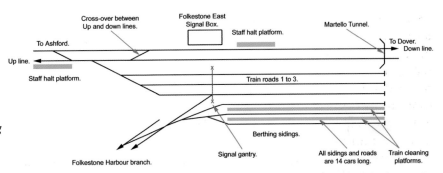

FIG. 2: The post-1999 track arrangement at Folkestone East following re-signalling of the location. Track formations are simplified and, in consequence, too simple for truly interesting operation on a layout.

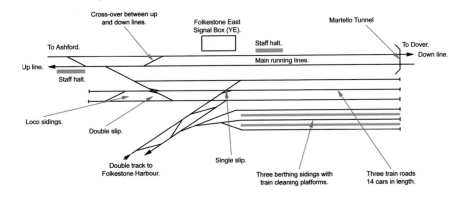

FIG. 3: The pre-1999 track layout is simpler than that when the signal box at Folkestone East was built, but still with too many complex features to suit my space. The double and single slips do little to create a low maintenance layout.

FIG. 4: The compromise between the two track layouts; my model assumes the simplification of the location when re-signalled was not as severe as that seen in Fig. 2. This will make operations interesting while fitting the given space comfortably with 1:6 turnouts and a diamond crossing.

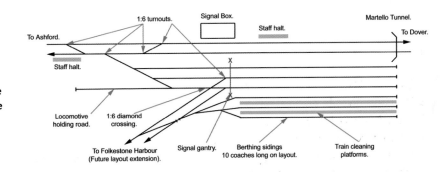

some 220ft of main line run to play with, equating to around 7 scale miles of track (excluding the 100ft in the helix). The answer was to close up the distances between some loops and not to include all of the towns on the line I am modelling, carefully selecting those that make distinctive LDEs to place the layout in south-west Montana. This is another form of selective compression.

Selective compression is possible within larger LDEs to make them fit. For example, the real Folkestone East has three train roads for reversal on to the harbour branch (depending on the date and track formation at the time) and three EMU berthing roads. Each is fourteen coaches in length (64ft long Mk 1 and Mk 2 stock), equating to a minimum of 900ft of track per road to accommodate three 4-Cep 4-car EMUs and two Motor Luggage Vans (MLV) in one train. This equates to 11.9 scale feet, excluding turnouts and the signal overlap. Far too long for my plan, if I am to model the junction where the branch diverges. I scaled the train roads back to just over 9ft in length, which enables me to squeeze in a ten-coach train or eight locomotive-hauled coaches and two locomotives, room for 'top and tail' operation.

Planning tools for successful layout design: prototype information, track plans, operations books and other such material are invaluable for designing the layout and deciding on layout design elements. It is worth seeking them out as they will answer many questions about your chosen prototype.

The system profile book for MRL's main line and branches contains a huge amount of valuable information, which I used to the full to design the track plan for the layout. Similar publications for all railroads are likely to be available and should be considered as an investment in the project because they are scarce and usually expensive. Check issue dates to see whether they match your time period, or the information for a given location may not be entirely correct.

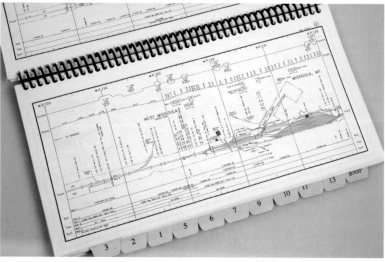

Turnout templates are perfect for visual track planning. If you cannot obtain such templates, make photocopies of the actual track turnouts you plan to use. They work just as well.

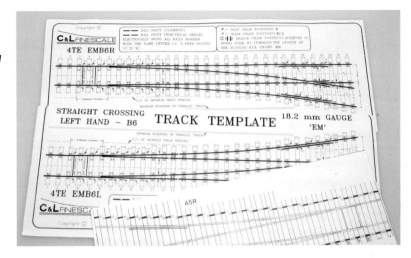

So be prepared to accommodate such compromises in your design, but bear in mind how they can be turned into an asset when it comes to scenery, doing layout photography and actually realizing your goals.

TRAIN LENGTHS

I have touched upon train lengths already when looking at selective compression. Train length is important for several reasons:

- Overly long trains can look out of context on a layout of a given size. The length of a train can be emphasized by the scenic effects placed on a layout without having to add additional passenger or freight cars.

- There is no point operating trains longer than your longest staging yard road or passing siding. Ideally, when planning the track layout make your passing sidings a set length and restrict the longest train to that.
- Ensure that your staging yard roads are of roughly equal length and about 15 per cent longer than the maximum train length.
- Allow for some overlap to give your operators room for error.

Sometimes, the performance of a train can be improved simply by reducing its length by one car, especially on gradients and through complex track work. While one of the objectives of my MRL theme is to run long,

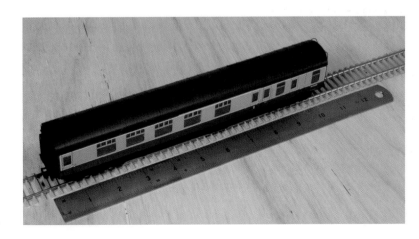

The standard length I used to determine train lengths and therefore staging yard road lengths on Folkestone East was a BR Mk.1 coach. The length of this model is the same for my EMU stock and the majority of the charter train coaches I plan to operate.

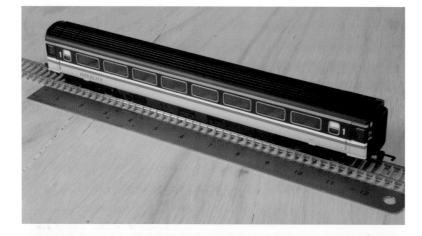

Unfortunately, not all locomotives and coaches are the same length. The BR Mk 3 coach is quite a bit longer than a Mk 1 or a Mk 2 coach, the difference being 40mm over the couplings, more or less.

It is useful to know the length of your multiple units. This information may be used to determine the length of bay platforms at stations. This is a Dapol Class 156 in N gauge which shows that this exercise is important for all scales.

heavy-tonnage freight trains; reliable operations form another one. When planning the layout and devising the track plan, make a simple list of the types of rolling stock you plan to run and measure the length of each to build up a picture of the possible maximum train lengths and the numbers of cars per train that will fit your plan.

MINIMUM RADIUS CURVES

Practical testing with your longest and likely to be the most troublesome stock will help you to determine the minimum curvature of your track for reliable running. This is an exercise I undertook for my Kato AC4400CW and SD70MAC locomotive models, following my experience on a layout with 12in-radius curves. These models, together with others with

similar bogie wheelbase arrangements, persistently derailed on the tight curves. It was essential that I should determine the minimum radius of curve at which these models would work comfortably without the risk that a single wheel would ride over the outside rail. I drew out, using a wooden trammel, various curves down to 12in radius on a sheet of plywood and placed flexi-track on each line to conduct my tests. At a 13in radius the derailments ceased to happen. At 15in the locomotives ran smoothly without too much overhang. I determined that 16in should be my minimum standard for the N scale layout.

This exercise proved to be truly worthwhile for my planning and a valuable one for you to consider. It can be used to check for buffer and gangway locking

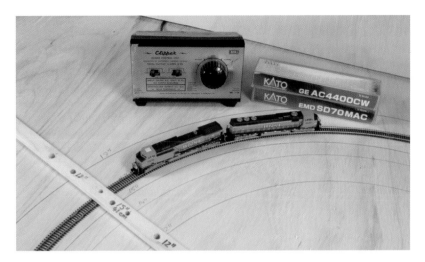

*LEFT: **Testing potentially awkward stock on curves, especially S curves, to determine the comfortable minimum radius of curve it will negotiate is an important part of planning and designing a layout.***

*BELOW: **To create curve templates to assist with design of the layout, use a simple trammel to draw out templates on stiff card stock. Label them carefully.***

and whether the coupling gaps between your rolling stock are sufficiently wide enough to run comfortably over the layout. When you have established this figure, do not compromise on it for a second when track laying. You may regret it later!

CLEARANCES

Just like full-size railways, our models have height and width limitations that determine the 'envelope' through which they can pass safely without striking anything. You must take account of clearance: take measures to ensure that you allow sufficient clearance between stock and lineside structures, particularly the sides of tunnels, bridge supports, signals and platforms. The same applies to overhead line equipment on electrified railways – have you allowed sufficient space between the top of your tallest vehicle and the contact wires? How about your bridges and tunnels? Will your tallest stock pass through without an embarrassing crunch? I undertook a series of tests on my longest stock to determine overhang on curves, and determine the correct clearances. The height of my tallest stock is checked with a combination square so that I can establish height clearances. For British outline stock, all equipment is the same height to fit the 'loading gauge', while US outline modellers may find that vehicle heights vary depending on whether the vehicle carries double-stacked containers or is a simple 50ft box car; refer to published data on minimum

clearances for model railways offered by the fine scale societies in the UK and the NMRA. The NMRA offers a useful gauge for several scales which provides a starting point in ensuring minimum clearance when planning and building a layout based on US practice together with its S-7 Standard, which may be viewed at *www.nmra.org/standards*. Generic British loading gauge information is published on the 2mm society's web site at *www.2mm.org.uk/standards*, although this does not account for modern loading gauge restrictions in the UK, which have to account for the carriage of containers of varying height and width on standard and low floor wagons.

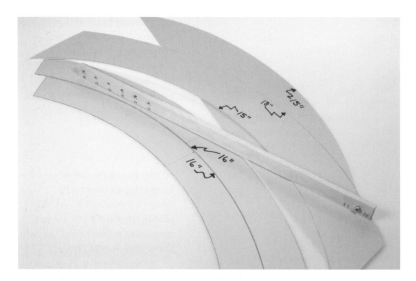

Here are the templates I used when planning and building the N scale layout. I found them particularly useful to check curves when laying flexi track and drawing out track centre lines on lining paper and the baseboards themselves.

Clearances for rolling stock are vital things to establish when layout planning. The longest locomotives and stock may cause clearance problems with structures, buildings and tunnels. It becomes more acute the sharper the curves; another reason for establishing a less than stressful minimum radius standard.

You really do need to avoid this kind of problem when you are designing a layout. Working out clearances is easy to do and can save a great deal of redesigning and track lifting in the future.

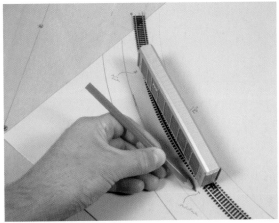

ABOVE LEFT: *Take your longest item of stock and some card stock. Draw in your minimum radius curves as seen in this picture.*

ABOVE RIGHT: *To establish the minimum clearance between running lines and structures close to the track on curves, the overhang is checked and marked into place on a diagram like this.*

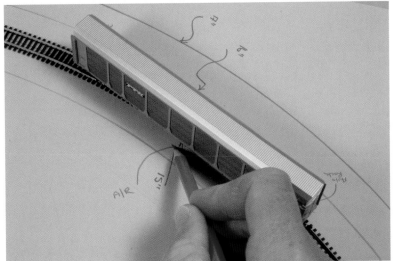

LEFT: *The overhang at the centre of the vehicle may strike lineside structures and passing trains ... mark it in too.*

The same exercise is applied to the longest locomotives to be run on the model railway.

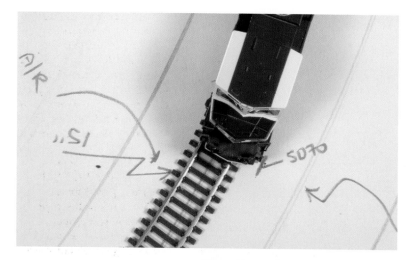

You quickly build up enough information to ensure that tracks are spaced sufficiently apart on curves to ensure that there is no contact between trains when they pass each other.

Place a second running line on the card, check the clearances and measure between the two lines. Any measurement will do as long as it is applied consistently. I measure from rail to rail so that I can use card spacers to help with track laying should I need to.

Check the height of your stock for vertical clearance – a combination square comes in very handy for such exercises.

LEFT: Allow for track and the track bed when determining the minimum clearance required for the tallest stock on the layout. Double stack cars certainly test the need for good clearances and the information gleaned from this process was used in the helix calculations.

BELOW: The difference in angle between a No. 5 (left) and a No. 7 (right) turnout demonstrates how the angle affects the length of the turnout and the severity of the diverging route's curvature. The distance between the switch (A) and the crossing vee (B) is clearly seen.

A NOTE ON TURNOUTS AND CROSSINGS

Turnouts and crossings are identified with a number. You will find modellers referring to a 'number 6' turnout. This is a direct reference to the turnout crossing vee angle: 1:6. For example, a 1:6 turnout has a diverging angle where a train travels 6 units of distance to diverge from the straight side of the turnout by 1 unit of distance. It is comparable to a gradient measurement in that respect. Clearly, a 1:4 turnout has a sharper angle of divergence, resulting in a sharper curve between the turnout switch and the crossing vee. A No. 10 turnout will have a shallow angle of divergence, resulting in a smoother transition from straight track to diverging track – perfect for higher speed running. However, this turnout is correspondingly longer and most inconveniently takes up more space.

For smooth operation, choosing shallow angle turnouts such as No. 6 (1:6) to No. 10 (1:10) or larger is preferable, but not always practicable, depending on the available space. The usual method for track planning is to use the larger turnouts in the scenic area of the layout and restrict the tighter ones in off-stage areas. The choice will also be determined by how good the stock looks when traversing the turnouts. If you have

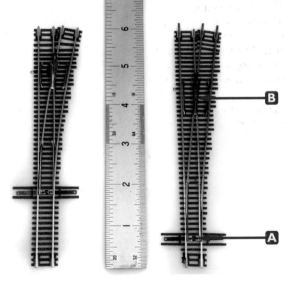

to use sharp angle turnouts, try to avoid the creation of S-curves.

The Folkestone East layout uses a minimum of 1:6 turnout angle on the scenic part of the layout and 1:5 in the staging yards. Tests demonstrated that all my stock ran comfortably through 1:5 turnouts, but they appeared unrealistic. While the 1:5 turnouts saved space in the staging yards, 1:6 turnouts and larger look far better on the scenic area of the layout and will be the minimum requirement.

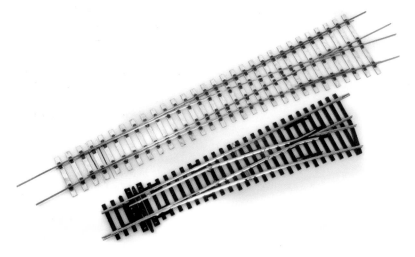

Not all turnouts are the same! This picture shows the difference between a laser-cut timber turnout that happens to be a 1:6 (or B6) and a Peco minimum radius point. One bases the diverging route on crossing vee (frog) angles while the other has a steady curve through the length of the turnout, even through the crossing vee, which is not prototypical practice.

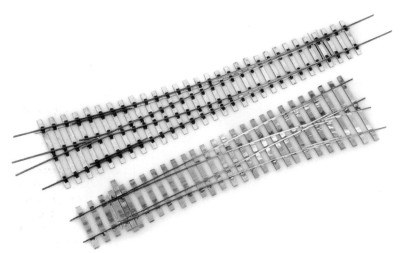

The difference between a hand-built turnout of soldered construction (a 1:5 frog angle) and the B6 (1:6 frog angle) composed of laser-cut wooden sleepers.

FIDDLE AND STAGING YARDS

In their simplest form, a staging or fiddle yard represents the 'rest of the world', somewhere for the trains to go when they have traversed the layout (see Fig. 5). Put in another way, the layout can be likened to a theatre, with off-stage wing(s) and the centre stage itself. If the centre stage is the scenic part of the layout, then the wings are the fiddle-yard areas. Hence my reference to off-stage parts of the layout, or non-scenic sections.

Fiddle yard design can take many forms, and, as demonstrated on my portable layout, can take the form of a moving or rotating sector plate, a traversing table,

or a simple fan of turnouts to access long storage sidings, as seen on my fixed layouts.

They can be double-ended with access possible from both ends (see Fig. 6), or as used on my Folkestone East plan, stub-ended so that entrance and exit are through one end only. Taking that as an example, I shall describe why I went for that design on the top deck layout.

With two staging yards, one representing Dover and the other Ashford, I saw that space and cost could be saved in making them stub-ended. This avoided the need to build six additional turnouts and provide all the wiring and expensive turnout machines to power them. By placing them to one side of the main running

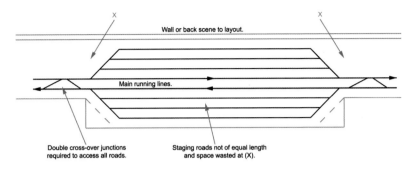

FIG. 5: *The typical staging or fiddle yard design employed on several layouts. It has stood the test of time and will feed trains on to a layout without any trouble at all. However, small changes to the design will save track, turnouts, switch machines and space.*

FIG. 6: *I considered this (double-ended) design for one fiddle yard on Folkestone East, but placed on one side of the running lines that would be pushed to the back of the baseboard. It would save space, and larger radius curves and turnouts could be included in the design as a result.*

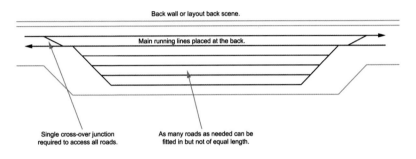

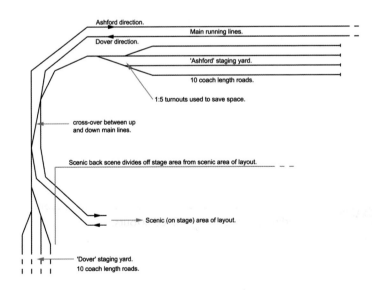

FIG. 7: *The final design of the fiddle yards for Folkestone East placed on opposite sides of the twin track main line and stub-ended. The majority of the trains running on this layout during operating sessions will be EMUs with cabs on each end of the formation. Propelling moves will be common as a result. With the yards fitted so that they face each other and connected by a cross-over between the main running lines, restaging after an operating session is made simple. Fewer turnouts are used to achieve the design and the cost is lower. The Dover fiddle yard is situated on the leg over the N gauge layout; the Ashford fiddle yard is sited along the back wall.*

lines, rather than by dividing the running lines in a multitude of through roads, as seen in Fig. 5, I could place them so that the entrances faced each other, with a linking cross-over between them so that both yards could be accessed from the double track main line (see Fig. 7). The same cross-over junction allows trains to be moved from one to the other without traversing the scenic part of the layout, easing restaging after an operating session.

Furthermore, the stock that will predominate on the layout consists of multiple units which can be driven in either direction. This further suits the stub-ended yard design. Locomotive-hauled trains can have the engine removed and placed at the correct end of the train or be backed into the yard after they have completed their runs, an idea I pinched from observing propelling moves into Vancouver Pacific Central station.

The fiddle yard must be capable of smoothly feeding trains on to the layout for efficient operation. However, resist the temptation to build huge yards to accommodate all your stock, because that runs the risk of the off-stage yard area becoming much bigger than the scenic layout itself. While this seems to be true of my Folkestone East plan, the yards themselves are narrow but long. I deliberately restricted the scenic section to one side because of the challenge of fitting a linear railway into a square room, as discussed earlier in the chapter.

The N scale layout has five long storage roads at the Missoula (eastern) end of the layout, which can be accessed by reversing a train on a reversing loop and them propelling it in ready for the next session (see Fig. 8). Alternatively, the five roads can be accessed from the far end too, making restaging easier. The type of train operated on the MRL layout makes double-ended staging a more useful feature than on the Folkestone East theme, making the additional cost more worthwhile. To keep the size of the staging yards to a reasonable level, I decided that trains could be staged 'mid run' in the passing sidings, because the full-size railway would not have had all its trains in a yard at the beginning of the shift. In planning the staging for this layout, I had

to have a short return line so that I could 'restage' trains easily between operating sessions, especially those that are 'one-way', such as loaded coal trains which run only east to west over the MRL 4th Sub. This is shown in the final layout schematic as a red line on the off-stage lines (see Fig. 9, p. 72).

So, while there is no definitive staging yard design – for every one is different depending on the type and design of layout – you should consider the following points:

- Train length: ensure that your storage and staging roads are long enough.
- Do not try to create on-line storage for all your stock, this will make the layout seem cluttered and the staging yard soon becomes bigger than life.
- Does it need to be double-ended or would a stub-ended yard do the job?
- Consider staging trains on the scenic section as part of the layout.
- Traversers and sector plates are great for small portable layouts and they save space too, however, they can be difficult to build.
- Avoid making your staging completely hidden by scenery, part at least should be visible unless you are prepared to invest in closed-circuit monitoring equipment.

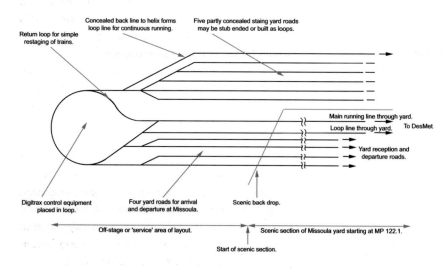

Return loop for simple restaging of trains.

Concealed back line to helix forms loop line for continuous running.

Five partly concealed staing yard roads may be stub ended or built as loops.

Main running line through yard.

Loop line through yard. To DesMet

Yard reception and departure roads.

Digitrax control equipment placed in loop.

Four yard roads for arrival and departure at Missoula.

Scenic back drop.

Off-stage or 'service' area of layout.

Scenic section of Missoula yard starting at MP 122.1.

Start of scenic section.

FIG. 8: A view of the eastern end staging and off-stage area of the MRL N scale layout. A reverse curve allows both propelling and forward access to the five staging roads. In the event, they were built to be double-ended to allow access from the opposite direction over the continuous running loop line. The turn back loop is great for turning trains for return runs.

RESTAGING TRAINS

The long main line run from one end to the other on the MRL N scale layout makes the restaging of trains between operating sessions quite a challenge. While it is fun to play trains running certain trains back to their starting points over the layout, it is worth noting that restaging might be needed during a session, which cannot foul the main line at any given time. Setting up a return route avoiding the scenic sections of the layout without employing too much extra or hidden track is a worthy layout and track-planning consideration.

Why restage trains anyway? Well, it is fair to say that many trains could be left at their destinations and run back over the layout during the next operating sessions. Tank trains, passenger runs and similar 'closed' vehicle trains do not show if they are loaded or empty.

However, how do you deal with loaded and empty coal trains, ore trains, ballast and aggregate trains? These wagons can be clearly seen whether they are empty or loaded. On the Montana Rail Link main line, loaded coal trains for Centralia and other customers flow west, empties flow east to the Wyoming Powder River basin. Those trains needed to be sent back to their correct starting points to avoid sending coal back to the mine.

Fig. 9 (see p. 72) is a schematic that shows the final LDEs selected for the MRL scheme and how the main line flows east to west, up the helix between the lower and the middle deck of the layout. Note both the return running lines on the middle deck from the west end staging yard and the use of the continuous run line on the lower deck to form a short cut line back to the eastern end at Missoula.

LAYOUT DESIGN

As suggested earlier, layout design is the process of fitting your theme and concept(s) comfortably into your given space, allowing for all of the givens associated with your particular domestic environment. Even an apparently dedicated layout space may have restrictions including services, head room and the need for other family uses such as recreational activities.

The idea of layout planning is to fulfil the following requirements:

- To ensure the design will suit your operators and, indeed, yourself as well as your locomotives and rolling stock.
- Plan for people as much as for track.
- Look at aisle widths.
- How far can you reach into a scene?
- Baseboard width?
- Height of baseboards.
- Storage solutions.
- Deck separation on multi-deck layouts.
- Access to inner operating aisles.
- Track bed types.

'SINCERE' MAIN LINE CONCEPT

An important design goal that prototype modellers strive to achieve is the concept of 'main line sincerity'. If the layout design is sincere it means that the trains run through a scene only once when traversing the length of the layout and that the layout design elements are in the order in which they appear on the full-size railway (as far as is humanly possible). The main running lines therefore do not loop around and through a scene more than once in a single journey as a result. This follows prototype practice, where you will observe a train approaching from one direction and watch it pass by, heading into the distance in the other direction. The concept is intended to enforce the perception that the train is going 'somewhere' and that there is a purpose to its journey. There are, as usual, exceptions where a prototype main line loops over itself and the model should do the same. However, this would still be considered to be a sincere model as the train would be seen on the same journey.

The MRL N scale design is sincere in that the visible on-stage main line runs east to west and from left to right through each scene once and does not loop through the scenes twice at any point on the scenic part of the layout. The sole exception to this rule is the second-deck, hidden line that takes the main line from the helix, along the back of the baseboards so that the scenic line can run to the planned east–west route when visible in the scenic section, it is a method to enable me to maintain the east–west alignment of the railroad. To make maintenance easier and for the recovery of any stalled or derailed trains, the hidden

If you are unsure of a suitable aisle width for your plan, construct a mock-up with tables and chairs placed facing away from each other, or with portable layouts, to see what width will be comfortable, as I am photographed doing here.

BELOW: Stick to your measurements when you have determined the ideal baseboard widths and aisle spaces. Place tape on the floor with measurement information recorded on it so that you don't forget. This aisle looks to be a generous 40in wide.

line is tucked away behind relatively low scenery so that a train's progress could be followed if required.

AISLE WIDTH: HOW WILL PEOPLE MOVE AROUND THE LAYOUT?

Avoid narrow aisles and minimize access pinch points whenever you can. I believe that to sacrifice a couple of inches of baseboard to make a slightly wider access to the layout is a very good thing. When operating on your own, narrow aisles may not be problematic, but bring your operating team round for a good session of running trains and long narrow aisles will soon frustrate the smooth operation of the layout.

The central walk-in aisle on my design is a whopping 40in wide. That was a deliberate design decision because the last thing I wanted was to have pinch points around throttle ports and control panels. In deciding upon aisle width, I considered how the operators would move around the layout following their trains, a process called roaming operation, a feature designed into the MRL layout. Another consideration is the top-deck Folkestone East layout, should that be in use at the same time: the Folkestone East layout does not suit roaming control, so the controls are grouped in one place, at the front of the scenic section. This effectively keeps the operator of that layout out of the way of engineers driving BNSF and MRL trains on the lower two decks.

There is a pinch point at the access to the walk-in aisle. This is located at the 'nod under' people

underpass where the top deck crosses the access point. This is still 24in wide and only 23in in length. The baseboard frames at the end of the peninsula are curved to ease access further.

So, when designing your layout, give some thought as to how it is to be operated and how people are to move around it, avoiding each other and avoiding the tangling of throttle cables. Radio or infrared throttles will help, but properly considered access aisles will be the key to success.

THOUGHTS REGARDING LAYOUT HEIGHT

How tall should your layout be? This is a personal consideration and will depend very much on a number of factors. Here are a few to consider:

How tall are you? This will determine the comfortable working height of a fixed or portable single-deck layout. Don't go too low! Making a single-deck layout about 60in high does not make it unworkable and may create opportunities to use the room for other purposes too.

But making a layout too low in height may make it difficult to work on and uncomfortable to operate.

Eye-level scenes may be more realistic and much more dramatic for your operators. Back scenes do not need to be as tall either because you are looking across the layout, not down into it.

Eye-level scenes mean that you may have to look at elements of detailing on your stock which you might not have considered in the past. Underframe detail and the way your models sit on the track suddenly become more important.

Is it safe enough for step boxes so that children and shorter adults can watch and operate a taller layout?

Allow for storage space under the baseboards.

A circular layout with an inner operating well may need a duck-under to access it; a layout of 40–45in high is going to be a pain to duck under, even if the duck-under section to the baseboard is very narrow.

Low baseboards can make for uncomfortable and unwelcome duck-under access to central areas of the layout.

Surveying your floor space to mark in layout baseboards, aisles and other features, including furniture, will help you to visualize how it will all fit together and whether your plans are realistic. That generous aisle became the central operating aisle with scenic layout on both sides, so avoiding a bottleneck was important.

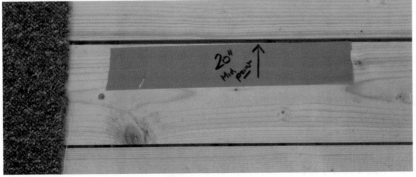

The mid-point of the free-standing peninsula was recorded on the floor too. This is a vital measurement because this is the line for the uprights that will support the middle and the upper deck of the layout.

A complete round-the-walls layout design calls for an access point to reach the central operating aisle. Tony Wright's 'Little Bytham' OO gauge layout has an ingenious lift bridge at one end of the fiddle yard to allow access through the exterior door. The electronics can be arranged so that when the bridge is lifted, trains cannot run towards it from either direction. (PHOTO: TONY WRIGHT)

LAYOUT BASEBOARD DEPTH – CAN YOU REACH?

There is a direct relationship between the height of the layout and how far into a baseboard an operator can reach. When considering eye-level rail height on tall layouts, the designer should take account of the distance that operators will be able to reach in to uncouple rail vehicles, clean the track or even do scenic modelling and track laying. In terms of layout design, it is a good move to ask your friends, those folk likely to become your operating crew, the best combination of layout height, baseboard depth and deck height for reach, comfort of operation and the provision of duck-under and nod-under access points.

Baseboard depth can be varied for other reasons too, even when reach is not an issue. A section of layout may be a shelf a mere 6in wide, because it represents a section of plain line in what will become a neutral scenic area between towns and industries. A narrow section of shelf layout can ease the burden of a duck-under. It is less back-breaking to duck under a 6in wide baseboard than a 36in one.

Scale also impacts on baseboard width: it takes a great deal more scenery and many more buildings to fill 20in by 6ft of layout in 1:160 scale (N scale) than it does in 1:76 scale (HO gauge). Buildings, structures and the permanent way will take up less space, so to fill a given area requires more time, detail and effort.

This, however, is one of the benefits of the smaller scale when modelling big scenery such as that found in mountain regions.

Some modellers in HO scale, OO gauge and O gauge deliberately model on narrow baseboards to allow for more aisle width and to limit the modelling effort to the permanent way and the land immediately on the side of the line. Usually, if operation rather than landscape modelling is the preferred theme for a layout, a narrow shelf layout concept, either on one or more decks will be designed.

MULTI-DECK SEPARATION

A big debate among layout builders is how far apart layout decks should be on a twin- or multi-deck concept. This is as intense as the debate about how tall an exhibition layout should be for good viewing by the public, and how high the first baseboard of a fixed layout should be for easy operations. Here are the key points I considered when looking at my multi-deck concept:

- The lower deck had to be tall enough for storage boxes to be put underneath it, but not so high as to push the middle and the upper deck higher than I wished.
- The upper deck holding the British layout had to be with its track at eye-level so it could be worked on and operated simply by standing on a stout, 12in-high step box.
- The top and the bottom deck had to placed so as to leave sufficient space for the middle deck, which forms the upper deck of the N scale scheme; the one advantage of this would be that it is at just below head height.

Note that in calculating the deck separation, I had to take account of the baseboard depth, including L-girders, joists, track bed and risers. One point regarding risers (the structural elements that lift the rack bed from the baseboard frames): when building a line on an embankment or across a geographical feature such as a river, the height of the riser may also affect your deck separation. Sometimes it is better to drop the height of the baseboard frames a little, particularly the lower deck, to make room for such structures.

The deck measurements used on my multi-deck concept:

- Height from floor to bottom of baseboards to allow for storage boxes: 31in.
- Depth of the lower deck from underside to top of joists: 4 in.
- Joists of the lower deck to underside of middle deck: 14in.
- Depth of the middle deck from underside to top of joists: 4in.
- Joists of the middle deck to underside of top deck: 14in.
- Height of rail level on top deck Folkestone East layout from floor: 71in in total.

THE BENEFITS OF DESIGNING MULTI-DECK LAYOUT AND USING A HELIX

Have you ever considered how much your layout costs to build? Per square foot? OK, OK! This means thinking about unpleasant things such as cost, when all one wants to do is play trains. There is a good reason for giving costs more than a passing thought. Beyond the price of timber for baseboards, cable for layout wiring, control systems, track, point motors and scenery, comes the cost of actually accommodating the layout.

To expand on the theme: are you planning to use a spare room in the house? How much does that room cost in mortgage interest rate or to rent annually? How much to heat and light? Add that to your area cost of building and maintaining the layout. The model railway may be housed in a specially constructed cabin (like mine) or a shed. Maybe the loft is your chosen home for your grand design. How much did that cost to build and finish, including an electricity supply? A single deck layout is only one layer upon which to calculate the cost. For a fraction more, the plan could be doubled by adding a second deck. Although the material costs increase for the project as a whole, the rate per square foot or metre will fall. You acquire more real estate, more running length and more bangs for your hard-earned euro, pound, kroner, dollar, or whatever you happen to have. More importantly, you make better use of that expensive space which you have worked so hard to acquire, certainly financially and also through negotiation with others in the household. The cost is almost, if not quite, halved for the layout scheme as a whole and metal shelving brackets sold in DIY shops take on a whole new meaning. Furthermore, you don't have to fill it all at once – build the layout in distinct phases to keep it under control.

WHICH TYPE OF TRACK BED SHOULD I USE?

Again, like most things in this hobby, planning for the track or road sub-bed is important. If it is to have numerous supports, the bed could be relatively thin, say as little as 9mm thick plywood. However, the greater the span between joists and risers, the thicker it should be; I used 12mm and 18mm thick ply on many parts of the layout. Naturally, I take the view the thicker, the better.

Once out on the main line of the MRL layout I changed to 'splines' for the sub-bed, a technique which involves building it from 4mm thick strip wood or similar. It is placed on end in long strips and glued together as a laminate structure. It creates natural easements (transitions) into curves and is better suited to long lengths of single track line than narrow strips of plywood. I did find it more expensive to use than plywood for long, straight sections of line, but it avoids the cutting of awkward plywood sections when creating curves, with all of the waste that entails. With the width of the splines on end, it is very strong and requires less support than plywood road bed.

Topping off the road or track sub-bed with the track bed itself is important for good running and the choices are many too, as usual. Cork of 1.5 or 3mm thickness is popular, with the thinner material generally being used with the smaller scales. It helps to create ballast shoulders and provides sound insulation. Also worthy of consideration at this layout design stage is 'Plastazote' foam sheet, a dense, black foam that really deadens sound.

My choice for the MRL N scale layout was the following:

- 12 and 18mm plywood for the sub-road bed in yard and urban areas of the layout, where the ground is generally flat.

- Spline sub-road bed technique in the hill country and rural areas.
- 1.5mm cork for the road bed in both the yard and main line track, placed over the plywood and splines.
- All track on the scenic parts of the layout is placed on a further layer of road bed consisting of foam tape 1mm thick, which saves the use of unsightly track pins.
- All off-stage track is pinned direct to the cork.

My choice for Folkestone East consists of:

- 18mm plywood for all sub-track bed.
- 'Plastazote' foam sheet 3mm thick for all track bed, both in scenic and off-stage areas.
- Track in off-stage areas pinned direct to the foam track bed.
- Track in the scenic parts of the layout is glued to the foam with some pins to assist the track laying. They are removed after the job is complete.

PLAN FOR CONTROL EQUIPMENT

With all of the sketching of track plans and thinking about aisle widths, layout height and so on, consideration should also be given to the location of control hardware. Where will you place transformers and DCC command stations where they can be seen and indicator LEDs observed? Will you be able to reach them for problem-solving and making changes once the layout has been built? Will all your wiring be accessible for repairs and fault finding? Where will your operators be able to place throttles during operations? Dropping them on to scenery is not a good idea and throttles cost money, so hitting the floor is not good for them either.

PLAN FOR LIGHTING

Multi-deck layouts have the advantage of providing natural support structures for layout lighting of the lower decks. Multi-deck layouts do suffer from the shadowing of the lower decks by the ones above, so more localized lighting is needed. My layout design allows for slim-line fluorescent tubes and fixtures that can be concealed behind the fascia of the next desk and suspended from a support frame above the top deck. I plan

Planning for control equipment includes items such as turnout machines. Are your baseboard frames deep enough to accommodate them?

The location of baseboard joists and uprights in relation to turnout machines can be determined by the track plan. One way or another, one should avoid the other. The position of joists can be planned in advance on paper so they can miss the turnouts. In reality, joists and risers are needed where support is needed and it is the turnout and its machine that need to be moved a little if the two are too close together.

Where will you place transformers and DCC command stations where they can be seen and indicator LEDs observed? I found the off-stage area at the eastern end of the layout, at the entrance to the staging yard and convenient to wall sockets, to be the best location.

for them to light from the front with an even light casting few shadows and without blinding the operators as they work round the layout. This may require the fitting of baffles and some reflective surfaces to redirect light.

The choice of fluorescent tubes is important too. The light balance and temperature had to meet my needs for natural photographic light which would be supplemented with light from photo floods, because the layout and all three of its decks will be used for photographic work. This may be an important consideration for your layout, so it is worth researching lighting temperatures and how the light will affect the appearance of scenic materials.

PLAN FOR COMFORT

The layout room is going to be somewhere that you might wish to spend a lot of time, both on your own and with your friends. I have allowed space for comfortable seating so my wife may enjoy her hobby work and spend time with me when I am working on the layout. When operators are between trains it is useful to have somewhere for them to sit, and to one side (with a drink) so not to be in the way of operators in the middle of driving a train over the layout.

Carpeting is a consideration too. Do you carpet the room before starting work on the project, which would be straightforward to do, or after it is complete, making carpet installation more complex? The former certainly would make carpet installation a breeze, but protecting it from sawdust, paint, glue and the other detritus of layout building would be a pain. Colour is important too. Buy a cheap, garish end of roll and the carpet pattern will detract from your beautifully finished layout. Choose dark, plain coloured carpet every time and find a paint colour for the fascia that will match the colour or complement it as far as possible.

BUILDING IN PHASES

Building my layout concept in phases was key to spreading out the cost and having some part of the layout operational to keep the enthusiasm going. Admittedly, it would have been best practice to complete all of the messy joinery first and follow that with a big clean up before a scrap of track, wire or a model train came anywhere near it.

However, to have something running on a lower deck (even though the track would need protection from mess when building on the higher decks) encouraged progress and also made it possible for my friends to visualize how the layout would work. Here is an outline of the layout phases I planned into the design:

Phase 1 of the MRL N scale theme:
track and controls fully operational throughout the lower deck including the peninsula; this includes the helix.

Phase 2 of the MRL N scale theme:
track completed and fully operational, including full controls on the second or middle deck, but unlikely to be anywhere near complete at the time of writing of this book.

Phase 1 of the upper deck layout:
construction of the two staging yards to support the Folkestone East layout together with the main line through the scenic area of the layout.

Phase 2 of the upper deck layout:
construction of the train roads and passenger train berthing sidings, together with the junction on to the Folkestone harbour branch.

Phase 3 of the upper deck layout:
building the Folkestone Harbour branch on a shelf layout concept around the far side of the layout room over the work bench and photographic table; it will be planned for construction in a couple of years' time and will have a main line run of 30 linear feet alone.

Phase 4 of the upper deck:
build a simple circular HO scale model of a North American location; the likely Layout Design Element may be Iowa Traction in Mason City, Iowa and its interchange with the I&M Rail Link and historically, Soo Line.

THE 'PROJECT PLAN' SUMMARY

Creating a top line project plan is an important way of deciding on the priorities for construction and where money is to be spent. The plan could have a timeline applied to it to focus efforts. As modellers, we are keen to have trains running, so this type of plan will help to achieve that objective, especially when there are others involved in the construction effort.

This list is an example of a high-level construction plan I devised to cover the period from the start of construction on 28 August 2008 to the end of 2009:

- Build the L-Girder baseboards around the two outer walls for phase 1; complete with baseboard tops in four weeks.
- Construct the helix to determine the precise deck separation between the lower and the middle deck; complete on L-girder frames in two weeks, including track laying.

RIGHT: A look at the top deck of the layout and the start of work on Folkestone East. This picture shows some interesting features including the cross-over between the two main line tracks (A). The cross-over turnouts (B) mean that the two stub-ended fiddle yards, one representing Dover and the other Ashford (in the background), face each other making restaging of trains easier at the cost of a possible bottleneck and the potential of conflicting moves at that cross-over. However, it simplifies track work and makes the yard roads longer to accommodate ten-coach trains, and propelling moves from one yard to another becomes possible without the trains' entering the scenic section of the layout. Another interesting design feature is the manner in which the turnouts are arranged to minimize sharp S curves between the main running lines and into the staging yards.

BELOW RIGHT: A look at the Ashford fiddle or staging yard on the Folkestone East theme with the main running lines to the rear of the baseboard. The fiddle yards are located on opposite sides of the main running lines rather than on the lines in the traditional way to create logical end-to-end operation in both the up and the down direction on the main line. Making the yards stub-ended means that they could be longer. Reliable stock and good track enables propelling moves back into the yards as required. The unoccupied baseboard frame to the front will be fitted with decks and sub-road bed for the planned North American HO gauge theme, which, at the time of writing (late 2009), was still at the planning stage.

A reverse loop incorporated in the track plan of the N scale MRL theme would enable trains to be turned at the eastern (Missoula) end of the layout for easy restaging. The track lengths to the rear of the baseboard were soon to become a staging yard for storing trains between runs. Trains could be drawn on to the reverse loop and propelled into the yard or driven straight in from the opposite end of the loop. In the end, the plan was changed to make those storage roads double-ended, with access from a hidden line from the helix back along the walls to ease restaging after an operating session.

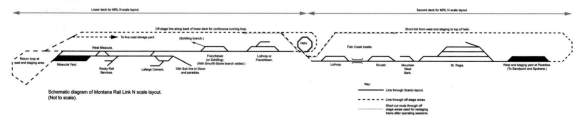

FIG. 9: The final track plan schematic for the MRL N scale project. Choices could still be made as to which scene of the layout could be used for Frenchtown, Lothrop and Schilling. Note the off-stage line running from the west end staging at Paradise to the top of the helix. This line represents only 6ft of track on the layout because of the way it was laid out on the peninsula and allows easy restaging of trains that should start their journeys from the Missoula end. The off-stage short cut is shown in red, a route that is considerably shorter than that when running the train back along the full length of the scenic main line – all 220ft of it.

- Construct the middle deck on the round-the-walls section and enough sub-road bed to enable testing of the helix; complete in two weeks.
- Lay track, including the staging yard and Missoula yard and install control equipment on the lower deck to include a return loop to enable operations to start on the N scale MRL theme, including testing of the helix; allow six months for the work, testing, bedding in and some time to play trains.
- Build the peninsula box frame (lower deck); complete in two weeks.
- Build the middle and the upper deck on the peninsula; complete in two weeks.
- Build the upper deck over the round the walls section, including the nod under for access to the middle aisle, enabling the start of a complete circular layout concept representing Folkestone East; complete in two weeks
- Build the staging yards for Folkestone East and the Kent coast main line through the scenic section to enable continuous running; construct, test and run over four to six weeks for fault-finding and bedding the track in place.
- Allow time for adjustment of rolling stock and locomotives to suit the new layout, its curves, junctions and gradients.

This plan was reviewed at the end of 2009 and the results used to devise the plan for the following year to include further construction. What each subsequent plan suggests could be completed will much depend on resources, time and money.

CHAPTER FOUR

TOOLS AND MATERIALS FOR BASEBOARD CONSTRUCTION

Tools and trains: the two are equally important in layout building. The design in this book required only fairly basic joinery tools, of which the most important were spirit levels and squares.

INTRODUCTION

What would the modeller do without the perennially useful Black & Decker Work-Mate? My particular example is quite old now, the veteran of many layout building projects. This piece of kit is supported by a variety of other tools I always have to hand when building layouts, and power tools are used to save time at every opportunity. I had allowed myself two days for the construction of the main baseboards for phase 1 of the fixed layout, and to achieve such an ambitious objective, power tools were a must. They included a cordless drill and power driver, a vicious-looking circular saw affair, which was equipped with a cutting disc suitable for ripping through plywood with the minimum of splintering, and borrowed from a friend. Another must is a goodly selection of spring clamps – lots of them – together with G-clamps. You cannot have too many clamps to hold work pieces together.

Steel rule, steel square, pencils, glass paper – all of these items are important, together with a good selection of drill bits, a counter sink bit or two and something to put them in during construction so that nothing becomes lost. My initial materials list for a layout project, either fixed or portable, included:

MATERIALS LIST

- 'No Nails' adhesive.
- Waterproof woodworking PVA adhesive.
- Hot glue sticks.
- Easy drive cross-head woodworking screws measuring 4.0×30mm (No. $8 \times 1^{1}/_{4}$).
- Easy drive cross head wood working screws measuring 4.0×40mm (No. $8 \times 1^{1}/_{2}$).
- Easy drive cross head wood working screws measuring 3.5×20mm (No. $6 \times {}^{3}/_{4}$).
- 12mm plywood sheets cut to 4ft $\times$ 2ft.
- 9mm plywood sheets cut to 4ft $\times$ 2ft.
- 6mm plywood sheets cut to 4ft $\times$ 2ft.
- Planed timber (dimensional lumber) 2in $\times$ 1in and $1^{1}/_{2}$in $\times$ ${}^{3}/_{4}$in.

- Planed timber (dimensional lumber) 3in × 1in.
- Planed timber (dimensional lumber) 4in × 1in.
- Dry wall framing timber for structural uprights for multi-deck layouts.
- Tempered hardboard.
- Sanding paper of various grades.
- Pattern makers' alignment dowels.
- M10 bolts, wing nuts and washers for bolting modular layouts together.
- Acrylic paint for treating the baseboards.

Let us take a closer look at choosing tools and materials for baseboard construction in more detail. This chapter does not deal with the finer modelling tools used to construct the track bed, lay the track road bed or the track itself, they are covered in Chapter 10.

CHOOSING TOOLS

Two things about tools, no, maybe three:

Power tools are the ultimate time-savers and the more you have to hand, the better. I would say that,

wouldn't I? As a typical male and power-tool junkie to boot, I can always find an excuse to buy yet more tool room equipment. Joking apart, it is amazing how much time and effort they can save when used correctly. Use cordless drills with quick-release chucks to make life easier and even consider buying a second one to really speed things up.

I stated the importance of my Black & Decker Work-Mate earlier. A good and solid work bench is essential.

Every modeller has a different view on layout building tools, so my list might not suit your needs. However, there should be agreement on much of what is listed here – the required tools are neither complex nor expensive to buy.

This is the list of tools I have used to construct virtually every layout I have ever built, including the fixed project described here:

Cordless power drill Absolutely essential for the inevitable drilling of holes and counter-sinking that comes with layout building. Make sure the chuck is a

LEFT: A useful power tool to have to hand is a high-powered mitre saw. It has proved itself invaluable for the repetitive cutting of timber blocks, such as those used to construct the helix on my fixed layout project.

ABOVE: A laser sight is built into the body of this particular type of saw so that the pencilled cut line can be accurately lined up with the blade. Very useful indeed!

quick release one, that the drill has good torque and have a spare battery on charge while using the first one in the drill so the work flow continues. They save a great deal of elbow grease too, because modern cordless drills are also highly controllable power drivers, capable of holding an adapter that will hold screw driving bits.

Power saws I use just two power saws. One of them is a circular saw which easily rips plywood into strips and it is a truly vicious piece of kit. Select a suitable

ABOVE: **This particularly vicious-looking piece of kit was used to cut sheets of plywood into strips 100mm deep for the sides of the plywood box frames.**

RIGHT: **When fitted with the correct blade it made short work of the job! Note that the cuts are clean and without rough edges, which would require time and effort to clean up with sandpaper.**

A hand mitre saw is a useful tool for cutting planed timber at almost any angle. While not a power tool it is perfect for incidental cuts and for those where more control is needed.

blade for cutting plywood to avoid excessive splintering and to make the job easier. I would never tamper with the guards on such tools. The second one is much more refined and is a powered mitre saw. It is perfect for cutting planed timber (dimensional lumber) into perfect lengths with perfectly square ends. My particular model proved itself to be invaluable for cutting the spacing blocks for the helix project described in Chapter 7. The blade can be adjusted to make cuts up to and just beyond 45 degrees. Again, the blade rotates at high speed, so do not tamper with the safety guards.

Power jigsaw perfect for cookie-cutter baseboard tops where sheet plywood or some similar material is cut to free-form shapes for track bed and landscape features. The curved deck segments used to construct the helix were cut by using a powered jigsaw.

Cross-cut saws are manual handsaws that are absolutely essential. They are useful for everything from cutting sheets of plywood into strips if a circular saw is

not to hand, to cutting hardboard and planed timber. In fact, they are useful for a number of different tasks as construction progresses. You will find yourself reaching for one at regular intervals. Apply a tiny amount of fine oil to the blade to protect it from rusting and to prevent the saw from binding when in the middle of a cut.

One very helpful handsaw is a manual mitre saw, which has been one of the most useful things I have ever purchased for all my wood-working jobs. Failing that, use a mitre box for making accurate 45 and 90 degree cuts in planed timber.

Hacksaws, both standard and junior, are great for cutting awkwardly shaped parts in both plywood and strip wood. They are close cousins to the coping saw which can be used for much the same purpose.

Measuring tools several tape measures, two 12in (300mm) steel rules and a combination square were to hand throughout construction. I also make my own measured trammels for measuring the radii of track

Drill bits come in different shapes and sizes. Three types of bit I am interested in using include:

1 A twist drill for wood-working.
2 A spade bit.
3 A twist drill with spade point.

BELOW: Resist the temptation to save time by driving screws part way into timber with a hammer. The accepted technique is to drill a pilot hole and finish the top of the hole with a countersink bit. This picture

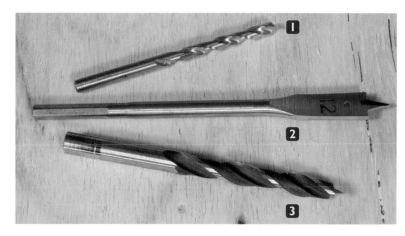

shows a variety of countersinks, including one which can be fitted to a suitable drill bit so that the pilot hole and countersinking can be done in one go.

curvature and to help with marking out of helix segments on sheets of plywood.

Squares essential for ensuring that the construction of frames and girders is square and true; I use both a woodworking square and a picture-framing square for layout building.

Spirit levels two types may be found in my tool box: a long one for general levelling work and a short 'Torpedo' type for levelling across short distances.

Clamps you need lots of these including spring clamps, G-clamps (called C-clamps in the US) and quick grip clamps.

Drill bits: have a box of different sizes to hand, including woodworking bits and spade bits for drilling larger diameter holes.

Forstner bits drill wide blind holes accurately with Forstner bits; a 25mm bit of this type is shown in use in Chapter 5 for the installation of alignment dowels.

Use a countersink bit to create a recess at the top of pilot holes to accommodate the top of a countersink screw. This technique is especially important when fitting baseboard tops.

A spade bit is used to drill wide holes of around 12mm diameter and larger. It is not suitable for drilling neat blind holes of any size.

A forstner bit is ideal for drilling neat, clean, blind holes.

Counter-sinks all screw heads should be flush or below the surface of any timber construction, especially baseboard tops and sub-road bed, where there must be nothing to make track-laying and road-bed placing difficult; uneven track will only cause problems now and in the future.

Counter-sinking bit combining both a drill bit and countersink in the same unit will save hours during construction; they are primarily used to drill pilot holes for driving in countersink screws; the countersink is done at the same time, saving the need to switch bits every time a pilot hole is drilled.

A handful of soft lead pencils have plenty of pencils lying around for marking out, measuring and general notes.

Vacuum cleaner suitable for rough jobs, including the hoovering of sawdust without becoming choked.

RIGHT: Screw fixings used on my layout construction including easy drive countersink wood screws with cross heads. Some companies supply the appropriate driver bit with larger packs of screws. Also useful to have to hand are bright self-tapping screws. Shown in this photograph are:

A. *Easy drive cross-head wood working screws measuring 4.0 × 40mm (No. 8 × 1½).*
B. *Easy drive cross-head wood working screws measuring 4.0 × 30mm (No. 8 × 1¼).*
C. *Driver bit and holder for use in a power drill.*
D. *Cross-head driver bits.*
E. *Easy drive cross-head wood working screws measuring 3.5 × 20mm (No. 6 × ¾).*
F. *Self-tapping screws.*

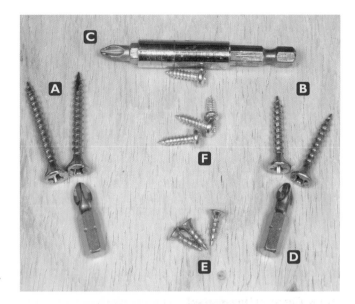

Squares are an essential part of keeping construction of layout frames absolutely square so that they will all fit together. A woodworking square (A) is the absolute minimum you should have in your tool box. Also consider a combination square (B) and a framing square (C) for checking large assemblies.

Don't forget a spirit level for levelling baseboard tops and other applications; the yellow one is called a 'Torpedo' level.

BELOW: You will need lots of clamps of various types, including spring clamps and G-clamps. You cannot have too many.

BELOW LEFT: Adjustable clamps are ideal for holding larger work pieces. They do not grip as well as the smaller metal G-clamps, however.

BELOW RIGHT: My trusty old Sure Form tool, which is the veteran of many woodworking projects. This is a super little tool for levelling off the joins between baseboard tops and pieces of sub-road bed.

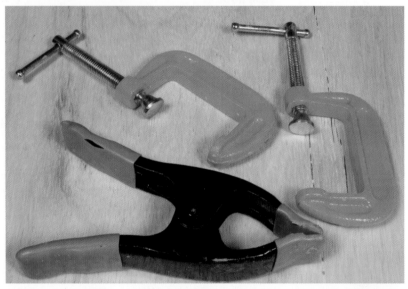

Sanding paper and a cork block should be on your tool list.

SELECTING TIMBER OR LUMBER

Buy timber and lumber well in advance of building day, and, on its arrival home, store the prepared timber in the location where the layout will be kept for a few days, so that moisture levels in the wood are even throughout. Furthermore, timber usually dries out after being taken indoors as most timber merchants usually store

plywood outdoors, if under cover. This will prevent the need to adjust baseboards after construction is complete. There are some things to look out for when selecting timber, and remember to buy the best you can afford:

- Look for excessive knots in planed or dimensional timber, they will be points of weakness.

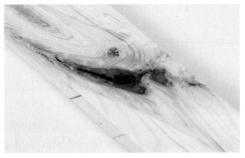

LEFT: *The bulk of the fixed layout frames are constructed from planed timber, also referred to as dimensional lumber in North America. Bulk packs offer value for money, but make the inspection of individual lengths difficult to do. Also note the nominal dimensions.*

ABOVE: *Avoid! Cut this out of a length of planed timber and discard because it is a serious weak point.*

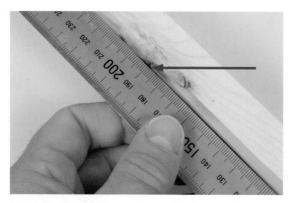

Knots also cause the warping of planed timber, undesirable in a layout.

- Look down the length of the strips to check that there is no warping or distortion.
- Check the ends of each length of timber for cupping, especially on pieces such as 3ft by 1ft and larger.
- Look for physical damage, such as the splitting of the ends and edges.
- Avoid rough-cut timber intended for exterior use. It is unlikely to be particularly stable and the cost saving is not worth the trouble it could cause.
- Buy timber from stockists who keep it indoors and safe from excessive moisture.
- While timber packs offer bulk prices that are better than those of individual items, the shrink wrapping may prevent close inspection of individual pieces.
- Examine plywood for signs of worm holes and damage, you don't want any such infection in the structure of your layout.
- Look for timber from renewable and sustainable sources.

ENSURE THAT YOU HAVE EVERYTHING YOU NEED

Prepare for your baseboard-building session carefully to ensure that you have all the tools and materials you are likely to need so that the work flow is not interrupted by the lack of a particular screw or pot of glue. Make a list and refer to your project plan. It is worth measuring up the layout space to ensure that the very minimum of materials are to hand to get the job on the move. One thing I learned in my baseboard construction sessions was: buy plenty of clamps and screws.

In fact, work out how many clamps you think that you will need and double the number. Waiting for glue to dry so that you can release clamps to continue work is a hold up in the baseboard building process. Finally, while it is tempting to use hot glue for construction, nothing beats good, old-fashioned wood glue for strength and durability or a modern adhesive such as 'No Nails'. This is why having plenty of clamps to hand is important.

BEFORE STARTING WORK, THINK SAFETY

Check that the safety guards on your power tools are functioning correctly and are not damaged. Use a Residual Current Circuit Breaker device (RCCB) on any extension leads just in case you accidentally cut through one. It may save your life. Organize your materials in a logical order so that you can pluck the required lengths of wood or sheets of ply from the appropriate pile and proceed with the project. This will prevent the working area from becoming cluttered and loaded with trip hazards.

The minimum amount of personal safety equipment you should use includes the following;

- Safety glasses.
- Vinyl gloves.
- Protective gloves made from tough fabric.
- Overalls or scruffy but strong working clothes.
- Residual current circuit breaker at the main power socket to protect against electric shock, should a power lead be cut during construction work.

Check the following before starting work on a baseboard project, especially if you need your tools to perform to meet the demands of extreme layout building:

- Power tool guards are functioning correctly.
- Equipment is clean and with good sharp blades and drills; discard broken or blunt cutting tools.
- Power leads are not damaged or split.

Read the instructions on the timber packs.
Check the origins and read the safety instructions,
such as those relating to cutting.

When selecting plywood, go for a minimum of
three-ply layers plus the veneer layer. The greater
the number of layers in your plywood, the stronger
and more stable it will be.

- Plugs and sockets are safe and without cracks or any other damage.
- Power leads are positioned so as not to trip anyone up.

SOME USEFUL SHORT CUTS

When fast-tracking baseboard building, there are several things you can do to speed the job up without compromising safety. For example, if you plan to use plywood box construction in the manner described in the next chapter on the construction of portable layouts, it is worthwhile spending some extra money and asking the timber merchant to cut the plywood sheet into strips for you. This service is usually available because quality plywood sheet that is best used for layout construction is sold in large sheets measuring 8ft × 4ft, certainly too large to transport in the back of the car. The price of each cut is usually added to the price of the timber, but it can save a great deal of effort and makes the journey home much easier. Choose the best quality you can afford because it will be less likely to warp and will cut much more cleanly than the exterior ply typically used for construction shuttering; saving you time in not having to finish rough

edges. Good quality plywood can be identified by the number of laminations, which should be of equal width, and the use of good quality wood. Don't hesitate to seek advice from the timber merchant.

Hot glue can be used as a permanent clamp to speed up the assembly of baseboard components. This technique is demonstrated in the construction of the helix described in Chapter 7, where hot glue forms the initial bond between pieces of wood, giving the glue time to harden over a couple of hours. The final bond strength will be formed by the wood glue, not the hot glue. I never rely on hot glue alone for timber-to-timber bonds.

Another technique to reduce the construction time is to plan layout sections to match the lengths of planed timber available from stockists. For example, I bought planed strip wood of 2in × 1in in 1.8m (5.9ft) lengths because the 1.8m span was well within the structural strength of L-girders constructed from the above-mentioned 2in × 1in. This saved me the task of cutting lengths of planed strip wood to size to make up the required length of L-girder. In the building of the first stage of the fixed layout, only a few cuts with a hand mitre saw were required and those were for the cross joists and legs.

CHAPTER FIVE

PORTABLE LAYOUT CONSTRUCTION

Platform 4a and 4b, one of my older portable layouts based on a 'bitsa-station' approach, is shown when under construction at the point where the track is in place and the scenery was to be started. The track was being tested and fine tuned by using the stock to be run on the layout when this photograph was taken. This small layout gives a flavour of main line action on small baseboards that fit in the back of a car.

LAYOUT DESIGN

Until now, all of the layouts I have ever built were constructed so that they could be easily transported in a car or van, exhibited at train shows and easily stored when not in use. One objective was to allow for house moves – which were always likely. Building permanent home layouts was not a practicable option for me for many years, given the need to be flexible with work locations. I did not fancy tearing out hours of hard work because job relocation forced a house move. Furthermore, space restrictions in the typical modern home suited an end-to-end layout concept, and I was usually in a hurry to construct them fairly quickly to provide a scenic photo stage for rolling stock and locomotives as well as an exhibition unit. A portable layout can be built and finished pretty quickly, especially if the frames from an older layout are reused to save money, assuming that they are in good enough condition. My small suburban electric layout, 'Platform 4a and 4b' was constructed on the baseboard frames recovered from an older portable layout called 'Mitcham'.

As discussed earlier, in the US modellers talk about 'givens' and 'druthers': givens being set parameters which cannot be changed and druthers are those items on the wish list that can be accommodated within the givens. A given for my portable layouts is that they have to be sized to fit in the back of a Ford Focus hatchback car, with no hardware occupying the passenger seat so that it is free for a fellow operator or Sarah (my wife) to accompany me to model railway exhibitions. By making layouts portable, I simply introduce more complications to the design and build than would normally be encountered with traditional baseboard construction for a fixed layout.

The benefits of building portable layouts are numerous and, for most modellers, they form the only solution open to them. First, they can be made to be modular, with standard fixings between each board and with each board being of a standard size, with the track centres at the edge of each board being absolutely precise so that the layout may be constructed in different configurations. Naturally, the electrical circuits must match precisely from board to board too.

Baseboard sizes could be 20in × 40in, 24in × 48in or variations on those proportions, creating domino baseboards that either fit end on end or side to side, and so on. It is a very flexible layout concept and one explored by modular-layout groups, such as N-Trak and Free-mo, in which modellers own individual modules, which they finish themselves but bring together as a group to create large and impressive layouts for exhibitions and club days. Details of the societies that promote modular concepts can be found on the internet, together with the specific standards for baseboard length, width, height and track centres. If space, time or funding are at a premium, a module may offer a way forward to the creating of a satisfying model.

The benefits of portable layouts can be summarized thus:

- Ease of storage, especially if a rack is built to accommodate the layout.
- Portability may suit those modellers that have no permanent space that can be dedicated to a layout; set it up, play and then dismantle in an afternoon.
- People living in rented accommodation can take the layout with them when it's time to move home.
- The exhibition circuit is a fascinating aspect of the hobby made possible by portables.
- Portable layouts may also be modular, assembled in different configurations if desired.
- Each board can be placed on a table or work bench so that it can be easily worked on for scenery, electrical work and track laying.
- One could be built as an additional project in a room dedicated to a permanent layout.
- Certain parts of the layout could be shared with others to save time, materials and money, not to mention storage space, such items could include the legs, lighting boxes and the fiddle yard.
- Portable modules constructed as part of a larger scheme may also be displayed at shows to showcase your modelling work.
- If the basic frame structure is not modified during the life of a layout, it could be reused for the next

project simply by replacing the baseboard tops and cleaning up the backdrop boards.

It is worth noting some of the drawbacks of the portable layout concept: a portable layout requires a great deal more construction effort than a permanent one simply because of its very portability. Each baseboard must match its neighbour exactly, every time the layout is assembled for an operating session. Electrical leads will need to have good and solid connectors between each baseboard and a method devised to support the layout securely – they are, by their very nature, free standing, so legs are important. Smaller portables may be rested on a table, but access to the underside if an electrical or turnout motor problem arises can be more difficult as a result.

There is a need to make them as durable and as strong as possible to withstand the knocks of being lifted, moved around and transported. Stable wood is required because even the slightest twist will cause problems at the ends of the baseboards and rails may no longer align correctly. Strength suggests thicker plywood, but then weight becomes a factor. But there are ways and means of overcoming these and other challenges to the practicalities of portable layouts.

If you can only consider a portable, it is likely that it has to be built in the home rather than in a shed, garage or basement. Make sure that its dimensions make it easy enough to manoeuvre through the house, and up and down stairs if needs be. Don't make the boards too heavy or bulky. If cutting wood in the house is likely to be a problem, consider building the baseboards out of doors and then bring them into the house for the more delicate modelling work. Time and mess may be saved in having the timber cut to size by the timber merchant rather than doing it in the house, with all the mess that can cause. One way of checking the stability of the timber you have bought is to lay it out in the room in which the layout will be stored for a few weeks before starting to build the frames to allow it to equalize with your atmosphere and humidity levels. Anything that twists or warps in that time should not be used.

In my case, the required fit in the back of the car established more givens in the design of my portable layouts: the baseboards could be no wider than 20in and no longer than 40in. I build them with an integral back scene support, which simplifies construction and adds more strength to the design for little extra weight. The concept I use calls for two long baseboards of 40in which are transported bolted face-to-face in a carrying rack. Two smaller baseboards of 20in length ensure that they will all fit in the back of the car, together with the fiddle yard. The layout is supported on a universal frame shared between all my portables.

The layout design is, by its very nature, compact and attracts a lot of attention at exhibitions because it demonstrates what can be squeezed into a small area without looking cluttered but with a high level of operating potential. One of my layouts, called Dudley Heath Yard, has two levels: the lower one depicts a yard scene, which is compressed simply to represent the throat and lead of a small yard, together with an upper level which has a single freight line and passenger line. The use of two levels increases the amount of railway action that can be fitted on to a compact layout for the price of some additional joinery but without the overall effect looking too crowded. The additional joinery to create a second level was worthwhile because it divides the layout into two operating zones so that two people can enjoy operations at the same time.

Pattern maker's dowels make excellent alignment devices for portable layout baseboards. They are reliable and secure, and absolutely necessary when a layout has to be assembled and broken down reliably, time after time. This type is supplied by C&L Finescale.

BELOW LEFT: There are many ways of joining baseboards together. I have investigated several with swift set up and break down of the layouts in mind. This method, using toggle catches, was found to be unsuccessful because it did not work particularly well with the support frame I use.

Hinges with removable pins are very strong and are my preferred method. Don't forget to take the pins with you when travelling to a show.

The suburban layout, Platform 4a and 4b, was equipped with only six turnouts but enjoyed the benefits of six fiddle yard roads, which gave it a great deal of operational potential. Although only 12ft long in total, it could keep two operators busy for a two-day exhibition.

Of the many techniques for baseboard construction, I prefer plywood box construction (also known as egg-box construction) where the frames consist of a box of 12mm plywood 4in (100mm) deep so that there is sufficient clearance for wiring and devices such as Tortoise point motors. The plywood sections are joined using blocks of 2in × 1in square planed timber, which are glued and screwed together for strength. The baseboard top consists of 12mm plywood, which is cut for the track bed, leaving holes where scenery will be placed or access to the underside of the upper level will be required to install wiring and point motors.

All cut wood should be sanded to remove rough edges and splinters because this layout is designed to be handled. Although I wear gloves when handling baseboards, not everyone does and your helpers will appreciate your efforts to make the job easier.

The support frame is of the same construction: 2in × 1in blocks of planed timber sandwiched between 4in (100mm) strips of 9mm plywood for strength. The legs are also of 2in × 1in which lock into the frames. Each frame is 40in long, one for each unit length of baseboard. They are linked together with door hinges fitted with removable pins. This frame also supports the lighting box too. The layout then sits inside the frames, resting on the cross pieces for each leg.

When you compare this construction method with the L-girder and box frame construction used to build my fixed multi-deck layout concept, where the use of glue was minimized to allow the relocation of joists and other support members, the construction of portables is all about glue and screw because modifications to the structural frame after its completion are not desirable if structural integrity is to be retained.

CONSTRUCTION TECHNIQUE

The following sequence of photographs shows how the baseboard construction for my Dudley Heath Yard portable layout was undertaken from raw timber to completed baseboards, together with back scene supports. The layout now resides in the same cabin as my fixed layouts, being set up from time to time in the space in front of the fixed layout's peninsula.

The first task was to cut 12mm plywood into 100mm deep strips. Lots of them! A great deal of noise and sawdust later and a pile of strips was available for forming the sides of each baseboard frame. A powered mitre saw was used to cut numerous blocks of timber into 100mm lengths for joining the plywood sections together. The sides of the frames consist of a sandwich of two lengths of plywood joined together with the wooden blocks. Modern adhesives such as 'No Nails' can be used to save time. But I still reinforced the joints with cross-head countersunk screws.

THIS PAGE:

LEFT: *Glue and screw is the order of the day: a generous application of glue is squeezed on to the plywood strips and a clamp secures the block in place before the screws are driven firmly into place. Countersink the screws for a neat finish.*

BELOW: *This image shows the construction of two short baseboards of 20in length. Construction is exactly the same: wooden blocks sandwiched between plywood. Note the use of clamps.*

OPPOSITE PAGE:

TOP: *This picture shows the basic plywood structure with the wooden blocks used to join sections of plywood together to create a strong baseboard frame. Cross members will be added once turnout locations have been determined. This board is a 40in long baseboard. Additional blocks of wood are fitted to the inside of the ends of each baseboard. This can be done with or without the tops in place. These blocks provide the foundation for pattern maker's dowels.*

BOTTOM: *The baseboard tops consist of 12mm plywood to further resist warping. Note that the end pieces of plywood used in the construction of the box are slightly deeper so that they will protect the ends of the baseboard top. The tops are screwed into place temporarily so the track plan and design can be marked in place on them before any further cutting takes place.*

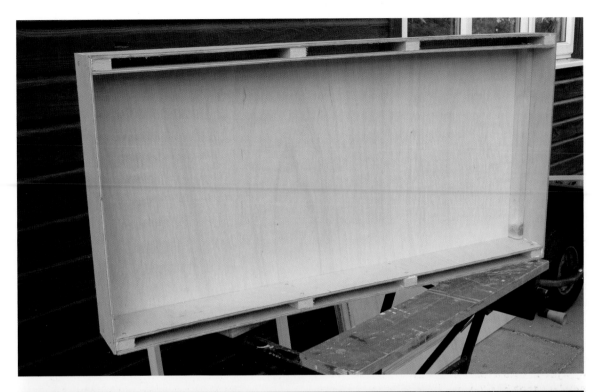

Work commences on fitting the back scene support boards that consist of 6mm ply wood. Strip wood is added to reinforce the back scene boards.

The main boards are placed face to face to work out how to make the end plates that will join them together for safe transportation as a single unit. The lengths of strip wood will be reinforced with plywood on the outside, avoiding contact with the rail ends and protecting the scenery.

A short fiddle yard consisting of a sector plate mounted on a simple plywood box frame baseboard.

The same fiddle yard board in use on the Dudley Heath Yard. It is possible, using modular techniques, to build parts like this to suit more than one layout, saving time, materials and money. The flat surface to the front of the sector plate will hold the DCC control equipment.

Portable layout baseboards can be made to be quite narrow and could form the basis of a shelf layout with each module removable so work can be done to it comfortably at a table.

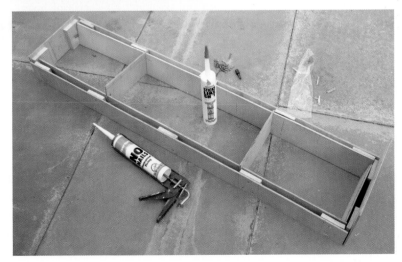

JOINING BASEBOARDS TOGETHER – RELIABLY!

For the newcomer to the hobby, the question of accurately aligning modular or portable layout baseboards is an important one. How do experienced modellers align baseboards, and therefore the track, accurately every time the layout is set up? After all, this is not something that visitors to model railway exhibitions will actually see, given that such systems are hidden underneath the baseboards and behind drapes and the setting up is done when public access is not normally allowed.

There is no single answer to this problem, which is faced by every modeller with a portable or modular layout. There are as many solutions as there are layouts on the exhibition circuit. In the building of Dudley Heath Yard, together with past layouts built to be portable, I always sought ways in which the layout could be assembled and dismantled as quickly as possible while avoiding damage to scenery and track.

Some modellers rely on simply joining the layout together with G-clamps and making the finer adjustments by loosening and tightening them, using the slack to inch the rails together and make sure that everything is correctly aligned. Speaking from experience when exhibiting my earlier exhibition layouts, this can take too long to do and is not foolproof. Another favoured method is to rely on large bolts and butterfly nuts to secure baseboards together and provide a degree of alignment. After a while, the holes drilled through the ends of the baseboards become worn and alignment is less accurate, thus resulting in the need for the same fine adjustment as would be required if G-clamps had been used. What is needed is an accurate and foolproof method of aligning baseboards so that they go together in the desired way time after time.

Ideally, alignment dowels should be attached to the baseboards during their construction and before any track is placed. This ensures that the baseboards align correctly every time and are stable, which means that the modeller can then place the track by using the preferred method of keeping it stable at the baseboard joints without the worry of being unable to align them accurately for the installation of alignment dowels.

There are a variety of alignment dowels available for railway modellers to purchase. They all have one thing in common in that they need to be accurately installed on both sides of the baseboard joint so that they can do their job. One type is turned from brass bar and consists of two parts: a bullet-like plug of about 20mm in length and a corresponding socket. They do not have a mounting flange.

Another popular type is a plug and socket pair, with a 25mm (or thereabouts) diameter mounting flange fitted with three screw holes. It is regarded as a more accurate design and is my preferred choice.

Some modellers make their own alignment system by using wooden dowelling, which is easy to obtain and relatively inexpensive. The disadvantage of wood is that it will wear over time, much more quickly than dowels turned from steel or brass. But if this is your preferred route, then choose a large-diameter dowel rather than a small one.

HOW TO PROCEED ...

1. Examine the end of each baseboard to be joined and identify where alignment dowels can be fitted. Ensure that there is sufficient strength to support them, sufficient depth of wood to accommodate the securing screws and that the dowels will not interfere with any wood screws used in the construction of the baseboard. Do the same to identify the location of holes to accommodate securing bolts.

2. Use a 2mm-diameter bit to drill a hole through the end of one baseboard only for each alignment dowel and each securing bolt. Choose the baseboard where there is sufficient room underneath it to get a power drill in place. Those first holes are the pilot holes that provide a guide to accurately drill holes into both baseboard ends and to align the Forstner drill accurately too.

3. The baseboards are carefully clamped together so that the track (if any) together with any scenic structures are accurately aligned. Double check the accuracy of the alignment when doing this because changes are difficult to make after work has begun.

For the newcomer to the hobby, the question of accurately aligning modular or portable layout baseboards is an important one. How do experienced modellers align baseboards like these accurately every time the layout the set up?

Mark in locations for the alignment dowels and securing bolts so to avoid existing fixings and screws.

4. Using the 2mm pilot holes previously drilled in the first baseboard and complete the holes by drilling right through into the second baseboard using the same 2mm-diameter drill bit.
5. Separate the two baseboards and examine the ends. You will notice the pilot holes drilled through both baseboard ends, which will face each other when the boards are brought together. Use those pilot holes to drill both the blind holes to

After drilling 2mm-diameter pilot holes, holes large enough for the new M10 retaining bolts were drilled through the baseboard ends. At this point, I decided to finalize the alignment of the baseboards with bolts rather than clamps before drilling pilot holes for the dowels.

Large bolts and wing nuts are ideal for clamping boards together. Don't forget to have spares to hand in case one goes missing at a show.

accept the alignment dowels and holes to accept the retaining bolts. The pilot holes will guide the various drills for accuracy, certainly as close as is possible on the workbench.

6. Fit the alignment dowels and test-assemble the two baseboards together, making adjustments where necessary. Use the retaining bolts and butterfly nuts to secure the baseboards together. Scenic features and the track will align as intended.

When working with a modular design, carefully check published data for baseboard ends with the relevant modular layout association or consider making a jig so that each alignment dowel and bolt position are the same and easily repeated for each module.

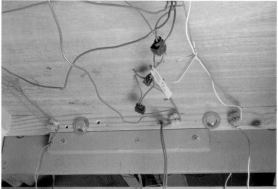

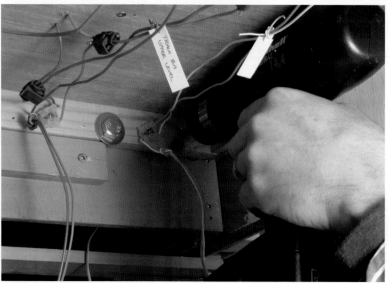

ABOVE LEFT: A sneak peek under the baseboard after the fiddle yard and first board have been joined showing the bolts, washers and wing nuts.

ABOVE: Another view of the underside; note the use of jumpers for electrical circuits and connectors enabling the baseboards to be separated.

LEFT: Drilling the pilot holes for the alignment dowels while the boards are joined together. Keep the drill as straight on as possible – not always easy when also trying to take photographs!

The pilot holes guide the Forstner drill accurately to drill shallow blind holes.

LEFT: *The corresponding hole is drilled out on the opposite baseboard too.*

BELOW LEFT: *Test fit for depth and also for alignment by using the alignment dowels.*

BELOW: *C&L alignment dowels are secured with three screws through the flange, which makes for a strong and durable installation. A male and a female should be opposite each other and the result should be an accurate and speedy alignment of baseboards, every time the layout is erected.*

SOME FINISHING WORK

Now the glue holding plywood and timber in the baseboards has hardened, give everything a good rub down to remove splinters and rough edges. Treat the boards with several coats of varnish or a coat of acrylic paint from a DIY shop – my preferred method. For example, a really good, neutral colour is 'Kashmir Beige' produced by Craig and Rose of Edinburgh under

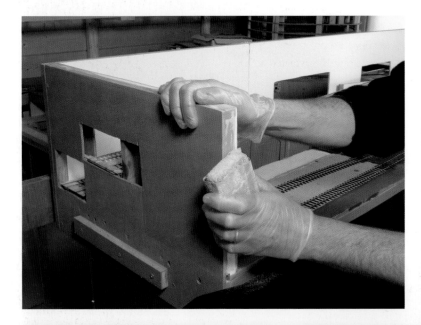

Finishing parts of the layout is important if it is to look neat and well presented when at train shows or when being displayed at home. Rubbing down with sanding paper also reduces the risk of splinters, which is important for a layout that will see much handling.

BELOW: Finishing with sanding paper will remove dust, brush marks and other imperfections from painted surfaces such as the back drop.

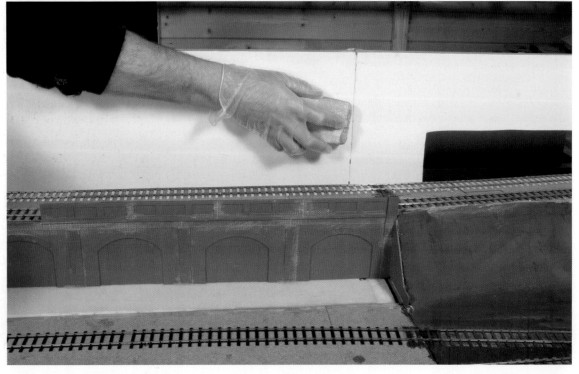

its authentic period 1829 colour range. This paint is water-borne, has little smell and dries to a very tough, durable finish, making it ideal for the fascia strip too. It is the closest I have found here in the UK to what US modellers call 'latex tan paint'. Varnishing or painting are both beneficial to protect the wood from damp and to further reduce the risk of splinters. Painting should be considered for permanent layouts too if they were built in potentially damp places.

RIGHT: *Coating the baseboards with a good quality acrylic paint will protect them from damp and help provide good presentation.*

BELOW: *Another scene from the Dudley Heath Yard; with alignment dowels in place, scenic treatment and the construction of large features can start; with you confident in the knowledge that the baseboards will go together reliably so that joins in retaining walls and track will align perfectly.*

NOW YOUR LAYOUT IS READY FOR THE ROAD ...

Experienced modellers have a routine that ensures that the transporting and setting up of their portable layouts are done as smoothly as possible. I have a check list of things I know that I must not forget to take with me. Some are absolutely essential to setting up and operation, while others may be needed but only in an emergency, such as a power failure. I hope that you find the list useful when starting out on the road. I also hope that you never need to use half of it!

EXHIBITION CHECK LIST

ESSENTIALS

- Layout legs, frame and support parts.
- Bolts, washers and wing nuts for joining baseboards together.
- Cloth drape to hide the legs and/or support structure.
- Lighting pelmet supports and the lighting units themselves.
- Control equipment.
- Any relevant signage, such as the layout name.
- Train stock boxes.
- Extension lead.
- Residual current circuit breaker (RCCB), sometimes required for some shows.
- Bar stool(s) for the operator(s) to sit on.
- Track cleaning materials, including appropriate fluids such as isopropyl alcohol (IPA).
- Wheel-cleaning tools, such as a scratch pencil.
- Locomotive cradle for use when cleaning locomotive wheels and undertaking minor repairs.
- Spare batteries for wireless equipment, such as hand-held controllers.
- Drawing pins.
- 'BluTack' or similar fixing material.
- Spirit level and scraps of wood for levelling.
- Back-to-back gauge to check rolling stock wheels.
- Track roller gauge to check track alignment should derailments occur.
- Coupler height gauge to check for misaligned rolling stock couplings.
- Control equipment instruction and trouble-shooting manuals.
- Something to eat and drink.

JUST IN CASE

- Modelling tools for repair work.
- Soldering iron and electrical solder for repairs.
- Spare parts including a spare turnout motor, wire and connectors.
- Crocodile clips.
- Adhesives and paint for repairing scenery and models.
- Spare scenery materials to cover up any accidental damage during transportation.
- Spare couplings.
- First aid box.
- A small quantity of the paint together with the paint brush used to finish the fascia should it be scratched.
- Spare lighting bulbs or tubes.

ORGANIZATIONAL ITEMS

- Paperwork and directions relevant to the exhibition you are attending.
- Maps of the location of accommodation.
- Risk assessment sheet – just in case.
- Layout description and data sheet with contact details should other exhibition organizers enquire about your model.

CHAPTER SIX

PHASE 1: L-GIRDER FOR AROUND THE WALLS

Track layout representing Montana Rail Link's Missoula Yard's west end reception and departure roads, together with the line leading west to a junction called DesMet will be built on the lower deck L-girder baseboards. Here is a view of the real Missoula Yard with a west-bound ballast working from Pipestone drawing up the main line. This yard is huge by British standards and modelling it all would have seen the layout disappear into the garden somewhere, but selective compression had to come into play on the layout.

INTRODUCTION

This chapter sees the cutting of the first piece of wood – the very foundation for what was increasingly looking like a very ambitious project. Work commenced on 28 August 2008 and almost exactly a year later I had about 95 per cent of the joinery complete and trains running reliably enough on Phase 1 of the N scale MRL layout to be able to host limited operating sessions with friends.

Baseboards are critical to the construction of a layout. They are the foundations upon which everything is built, even though their construction is not strictly railway modelling but something sitting firmly in the realms of joinery – something I do not enjoy as much as track laying and scenery. Nonetheless, they are vital in providing a solid foundation for that subsequent modelling, including the creative work we all enjoy such as the scenery, track laying, structures and landscaping. Get them wrong and a great deal of effort and work may be

lost. However, you do not need to have sophisticated joinery skills to build good baseboards – my skills are far from cabinet-grade standard. Furthermore, baseboard construction should not take too long to complete. Although taking your time over baseboards will ensure that a good job is done, there are useful time-saving techniques one can use to save a great deal of time and many of those are described in the following chapters.

Phase 1 of the twin-deck US outline project, the MRL 4th Subdivision main line, was to build the first level of the layout which would host the MRL main line from Missoula Yard to the bottom of the helix, ready for the climb to the second deck of the layout. This represents some 30 miles of main line, selectively compressed, of course. The line runs along the back south wall, curving round along the west wall of the building, past the site of the helix at about 45 degrees and round on to a two-sided peninsula which runs back into the room, extending the main line by about another 30ft.

Another view of the railway that inspired my layout theme: MRL SD70ACe locomotives together with a single SD45 switch freight cars in the yard at Garrison, Montana.

The two full sides of the lower deck running along the back and the side wall, together with about 10ft of the third wall, were all constructed by using L-girder bench work techniques for speed, economy and strength. The free-standing peninsula was constructed by using open frame baseboards, as experience has shown this to be more stable for free-standing structures. Bear in mind that the peninsula boards also have to support the middle and the upper deck of the layout, even though they will consist of relatively narrow shelves – a subject covered in Chapter 9. A single-

deck layout peninsula could easily be constructed by using L-girder construction if required, but be aware of the stability issue if second and subsequent decks are added.

I gave consideration to the following when constructing this round-the-walls phase of the project:

- When using L-girders built from 2in × 1in planed timber, no span could exceed 1.8m or roughly 6ft without a supporting leg.
- Joists to be of 2in × 1in timber.

Looking back on Phase 1, with the Missoula Yard throat straight ahead on baseboards against the back wall and the west-bound main line running towards the camera to the right on boards fixed to the side wall.

- The bench work had to be strong enough to support my weight over the legs because there may be a need to stand on it when working on the second and the third deck.
- Joists are screwed but not glued in place so, should there be a need to move them, they could be relocated easily. Ideally, good track planning should avoid any conflict between joists and turnout motors and other operational equipment.
- Would I have enough screws to hand to complete all of the lower deck area without an unwanted break to buy more?

Work began on the round-the-walls part of the layout first using L-girder, and it is this quick and very useful layout technique that is described in this chapter – mostly in photographs.

THE L-GIRDER CONCEPT

When building fixed baseboards like this, you are, in effect, building tables. The technique is simple: construct tables of a given length and join them together to create the desired length of baseboard. L-girders are simply that: the long structural members composed of two pieces of timber glued and screwed to form an L-shaped piece, which is usually very strong. The longer the span the girder has to cross unsupported, the deeper the main section should be.

For example, I decided upon three tables per side, of slightly varying length to span the length and width of my building. With three tables together with two bespoke ones for the helix and the end of the yard, the longest unsupported span would work out at just short of 6ft. To support this, L-girders of 3in × 2in were more than strong enough and were made by screwing two lengths of 2in × 1in timber together in an L-shape. I took advantage of the 180cm-long timber packs from my local supplier to avoid waste and having to make too many cuts with my manual mitre saw.

Increase the length of the span to 8 or 9ft and the combination should be a planed length of timber measuring 3in × 1in for the vertical section, fitted with a flange of 2in × 1in. Spans any longer than 9ft will require the strength of 4in × 1in timber for the vertical element. The L-girder would then be assembled into a table with the deep section positioned vertically.

L-girders are made into tables of the desired width with joists fitted at right angles at each end, where the

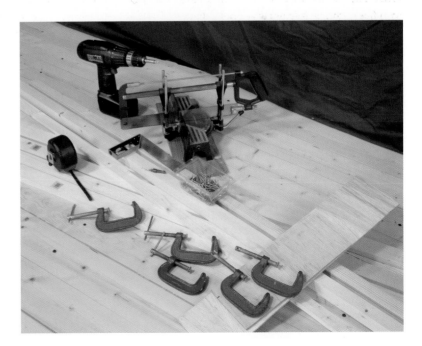

The basic tools and materials I used for building L-girders, including lots of clamps, 4 × 40mm wood screws, a mitre saw, wood glue, tape measure and drilling tools.

Basic principles of the L-girder: two pieces of planed timber glued and screwed together at right angles like this, effectively creating a flange and a deep section.

The girders for most of my tables were 6ft (180cm) in length and consisted of 2in × 1in planed lengths of timber. Note how the flange is offset from the vertical section. This makes joining L-girders together so much easier, with a very strong resulting joint.

Label each girder as you build it. The number relates to the actual baseboard table and whether it is to be located to the front or the back of the baseboard table.

legs will be fitted using 2in × 1in planed timber. The flange in the L-girder provides a very useful and secure fixing point for the screws. Further joists can be fitted to the table as required, as many as are deemed necessary to support the baseboard deck or top.

Apart from the end joists which are necessary to build a square structure, the other joists can be angled or fitted at right angles to the girders as required to suit the position of roads, rivers and so on. The location of joists can be adjusted to clear the position of turnout machines (point motors), if desired. I learned quickly not to use both glue and screws when fitting joists. You can guarantee that the joist you need to move is the one that you used glue to secure. Some parts of the layout have glued and screwed joists and they are located under the yard at the eastern end of the main line at Missoula. The plan was for plain track to be laid in those locations and the assumption that moving the joists was unlikely to be required.

Legs are added using 2in × 2in planed timber and braced with ¾ × ½in strips (or similar) fitted diagonally across the ends. Gusset plates of plywood off-cuts may be used to brace the legs further, if so desired.

Once a table was completed, it was moved into place and joined to the previously fitted one. Note that when you look at the photographs of L-girders, how the two strips of timber are fitted offset from each other. This allows the girders to be easily joined, and some additional pieces of wood will add strength to the structure.

CERTAIN CONSIDERATIONS

When planning my L-girder tables, I had to think about some measurements and how my choice of girder size would affect the final result. For example, I opted for short spans and relatively narrow girder sections so that I could minimize the overall depth of the baseboard structure to about 5in – sufficient for turnout machines and wiring, but so deep as to affect the separation of the layout decks. The deeper the girder section for a given height of baseboard top for the lower deck, the less headroom under the tables there would be for storage. Lift the tables up for clearance and that affects the separation between the lower and the middle deck. It is all a carefully considered compromise, and a balance in all aspects of layout building has to be struck somewhere. I could have used fewer legs and longer spans if my L-girder depth were 4in, but stacking five plastic storage boxes underneath those baseboards built along the walls would have been difficult.

The following sequence of photographs shows how I built my L-girder tables and fitted them to the walls.

Joists of 2in by 1in timber are fitted to the ends of the L-girders to create a frame. Note the use of a square. Clamps hold everything in place while screws are driven into the joist through the horizontal flange of the girder. Note that the flanges face the same way and are positioned facing towards the room both to the rear and the front to make the installing of screws so much easier.

TOP: *A completed frame ready for legs. Although it is shown with three joists fitted, more can be added as required to support the baseboard tops or track bed. The length at which the joists overhang the girders can vary depending on the desired fascia shape and the location of the table in the overall plan.*
ABOVE LEFT: *Legs of 2in × 2in timber are fitted to the end of the table top frame and braces are used to keep everything square.*
ABOVE RIGHT: *That's me again, in more disreputable clothing, securing the leg braces with screws. The legs could be strengthened if required with gusset plates made from metal or pieces of plywood.*

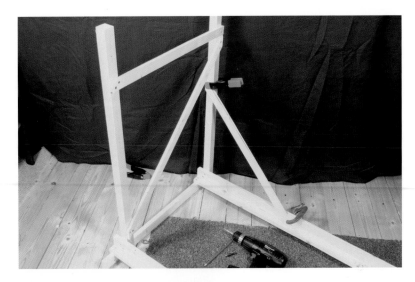

More bracing, this time on a different plane to keep everything rigid. Note how the L-girder flange provides a convenient fixing point, one of the many benefits of this type of construction.

A simple gusset plate of 9mm plywood can be used as a leg brace if the longer ones shown earlier cause problems.

This shows how the gusset plate works with the legs, joist and L-girders. It is a neater method than using braces. The size of the gusset plate may be varied, depending on the depth of the L-girder.

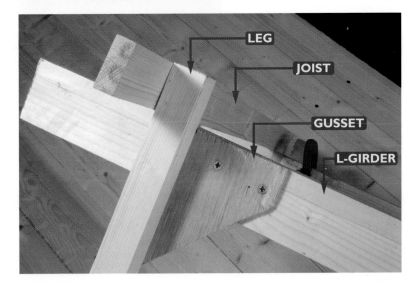

LEG

JOIST

GUSSET

L-GIRDER

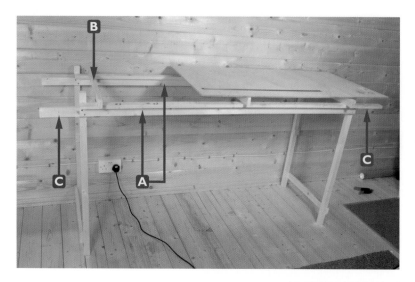

A completed table ready of installation. Features to note are the L-girders with flanges facing the room (A) and the joists (B). This picture shows how the top and side pieces of each girder are fitted offset from each other to provide a fixing point for joining to adjacent tables (C).

The assembling of the tables was well under way by the time this picture was taken. Solid baseboard tops were preferred for this area as it will be the location of the Missoula Yard. Storage under the baseboards is an important requirement, given my liking for building small, portable layouts too. As an aside, I use spirit levels during every stage of building – they are always to hand.

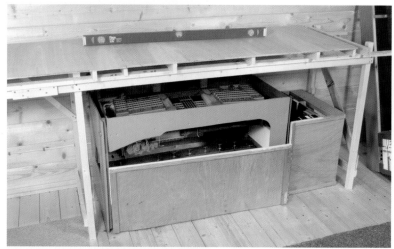

Joining the tables together by overlapping the L-girders together and fitting an additional plate across the join for added durability. Everything is held with clamps until screws can be driven into place.

Another view of how the tables are joined together along the girders.

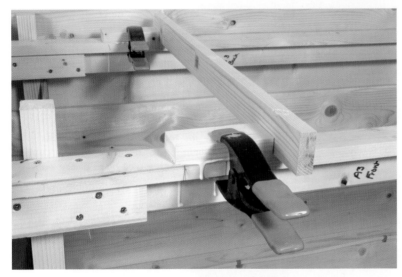

Belt and braces: another block of wood on the top of the girders and that join is never going to move.

Wipe those glue spills away, especially if they are likely to drip on to tools, materials, carpet or a wooden floor.

The location of the joists is drawn on the baseboard top so that screw holes can be drilled accurately. There's nothing worse than missing the joist with a drill.

LEFT: Glue was used in addition to screws to secure the baseboard tops in the Missoula Yard area, as it was unlikely that they would need to be removed.

BELOW LEFT: Simple wooden brackets secure the L-girder frames to the wall to improve stability. This was easy for me to do with a wooden building. If you are working in a brick or block-built structure, possibly with dry wall lining, wall plugs or dry wall fixings will be required.

RIGHT: Three spans of L-girder were used along the side wall, the fourth, smaller baseboard frame being of a different size and shape to support the helix.

A couple of additional joists can be added to the legs for simple shelving. This area is used to store rolling stock boxes which would otherwise get in the way.

Additional support joists are simple to add to this type of structure. Clamp the 2in × 1in timber in place and drive fixing screws up through the flange of the L-girder.

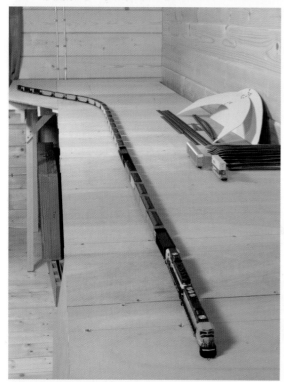

ABOVE: **The size and the width of baseboard frames are easy to adjust with L-girder construction. This is the end board located on the back wall, which will support the turn-back loop in the lower staging area of the layout – in effect, the east end of the line. An extra L-girder was added for additional width and longer joists were installed too. This board is 36in wide.**

LEFT: **To put the baseboard work into perspective: here is a view along the Missoula Yard section of the layout towards the turn back loop end of what will be an off-scene and service area of the layout. The yard is flat, so large pieces of 12mm thick plywood make up the table top and track bed. They are screwed direct to the joists.**

RIGHT: **Remember the setting out of the room discussed in the second chapter? A plumb line is used to check that I have built to my plans and that the layout meets at its special limits. This ensures that aisle widths are preserved.**

A smaller frame links the baseboard located along the walls with the peninsula (when it has been built).

Leaving a slight overlap of the timber used to make the L-girder makes it easier to join one frame at right angles to another. Note how they fit together, with the L-girder of the linking frame fitting neatly against the flange of the other.

Additional strength is imparted to the join by fitting a plate over the top.

RISERS, BASEBOARD TOPS AND TRACK BED

The beauty of this type of baseboard construction is its versatility. While not ideal for portable layout construction, it is solid enough even to stand on if the correct L-girder size and span length are used. Locating joist positions is simple: put in enough to support the track bed and place them so that they will not clash with turnout motors. Do not glue and screw them to the L-girder just in case you need to reposition one. When construction in that area of the layout is complete, the fascia boards may be attached to the ends of the joists, and creating curved fascia is easily done by varying the overhang length of the joists.

Risers are those blocks of wood that support the track bed if it is not to be attached direct to the joists. This introduces gradients where the track bed can rise and fall above the level of the joists. There are several ways of making and fixing risers, and they will appear in different forms throughout the book. In some areas, where the track bed is level, I use offcuts of 2in × 1in strip wood screwed to the joists after the correct height of the track bed has been determined.

Where inclines or gradients are required, attach the joist to the pieces of plywood making up the track bed first and then clamp to the joists temporarily until the gradient can be determined. This same technique was used to determine the gradient of the helix over its first full turn.

Things are moving along very nicely as this photograph shows. It looks complicated at first glance. However, you can see the two L-girder frames with joists already installed (B) placed at right angles to each other, one now has the helix stacked on it. A diagonal L-girder (A) links both frames together with joists positioned at 45 degrees and will form a route for the main line across the front of the helix. Risers (C) are in the process of being attached to the joists, shown here being held in place with red G-clamps until screws are driven into place. Track bed is also shown installed (D) in places as this area of the layout is developed.

Risers can be made from plywood too, cut to the width of the track bed itself, secured with a block of wood and fixed to the joists after any gradient has been determined. I discovered that there are a multitude of ways of making risers depending on the offcuts of usable timber and plywood that may be to hand at the time. As long as it is secure and even, don't be worried about having a different type of riser at each stage of the layout if it uses up stray pieces of wood.

A narrow track bed is fitted to the risers along the base of the helix. This will be an off-stage line that kicks back from the base of the helix to the staging yards for easy restaging of trains after an operating session. Again, the plywood trackbed, together with the supporting risers, are clearly seen. If additional support is required, another joist may be added as long as it does not interfere with the location of turnout motors.

RIGHT: *An example of a plywood riser: A: plywood cut to the width of the track bed; B: block required to connect the track bed securely with the riser; C: screws are used as track bed fixings; D: joist; E: L-girder; F: track bed (also called sub-road bed or sub-track bed).*

This is the view along the side (west) wall of the layout building, looking west along the main line towards DesMet Junction and the helix frame seen in the earlier photograph. The cloth drape is temporary – something more permanent to hide those items stored under the layout will be made when construction is complete.

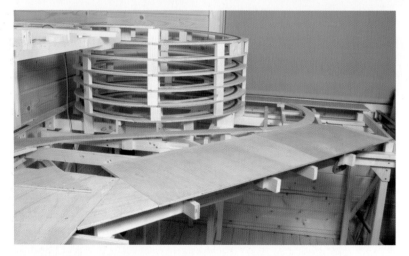

Don't be tempted to do finishing work with carpet and drapes until the messy work is complete.

LEFT: *All of those joists and girders are hidden under the deck of the layout, which is installed with screws in countersink holes so that the top of the board remains flat. This part of the layout represents some flat(ish) ground, so larger pieces of 12mm ply wood are used at the track bed and the foundation for the surrounding country.*

LOOKING AHEAD ...

As much as L-girder construction worked for the wall section of the lower deck, I was considering something quite different for the free-standing peninsula, partly to try a different construction technique and partly for additional stability to support two independent layout decks. This would be attached to the end of the short frame adjacent to the helix. Oh yes, that helix – it was time to construct that on its frame before tackling the peninsula. The next chapter shows how I calculated its size and shape, together with the methods used to build it. That was an exciting project in its own right as it would be a critical tool in extending the length of the N scale layout's main line!

CHAPTER SEVEN

CONNECTING DECKS WITH A HELIX

A helix is a delicate balance between gradient, track radius, the separation of the decks, the area of the circle occupied by the helix and the amount of track in each turn. In other words, is the helix a practical proposition for the trains to be run up and down it, such as this thirty-car coal train? Will it fit your layout space?

INTRODUCTION

As a piece of joinery goes, this has to be the most complex piece of layout construction I have ever tackled, so why does it appear at this stage of construction of the layout? The reason is simple: a helix is best planned and incorporated into the layout build at an early stage so that the exact height of the second deck can be easily determined and that the rest of building Phase I of the MRL N scale layout could commence with it

A good example of a helix constructed of 9mm plywood deck separated by threaded rods. While a very solid form of construction, the use of rods makes the setting up of an even gradient over the length of the helix run quite challenging. This one is seen in use on the Inverness and District MRC N scale layout.

in place, allowing for its size and height. This project within a project was thought through and planned on paper over many months before the first saw cut was made. I dug deep into schoolboy mathematics to calculate radii, areas of the circle, gradients and so on. Amazingly, there are modellers who actually construct two of these potentially space-eating monsters to enable a main line run to extend continuously over two levels of a layout. OK, I admit that after building the first, a second one did appeal to me. However, would that have introduced a great deal more complexity into an already ambitious project, I hear you say? One is complex enough, so why did I build it for the MRL N scale layout, and why is it so central to the design of that part of the layout? I shall explain why it offered so much in the way of benefits.

FITTING A HELIX INTO THE LAYOUT CONCEPT

The MRL N scale main line theme and layout concept revolves around a linear point-to-point layout with a very long main line run to achieve the best results from operations. With the operating plan allowing for trains of up to 10ft in length and a main line playing host to more than one long train at a time, not necessarily running in the same direction, trains meeting at passing

loops will be commonplace, sometimes involving lengthy waits for a train approaching from the opposite direction to pass. Digital Command Control will have a major role to play in such operations in providing for three or four locomotives assigned to a train, authentic lighting control, sound and realistic driving practice. An operator is assigned a train and will drive it over this point-to-point railway until it reaches its destination. A run could take over 45 actual minutes, if not longer, by the time meets, speed restrictions and other operational challenges are overcome.

To achieve that length of main line in my layout building I quickly realized that a twin-deck layout concept for the MRL N scale project was not only desirable but absolutely necessary. The design evolved into a massive scheme with 250-plus feet of main line, excluding the staging yard roads, freight yard sidings and passing loops. That's a scale running length of 10km or over 6 miles, excluding the calculated track distance in the helix.

WHY I CHOSE A HELIX OVER OTHER METHODS

As I planned my double-deck layout concept along came the challenge of how to link the lower and the upper deck. One method I considered was a gradual

Another view of the helix showing a sizeable freight descending the incline. Care is needed so as not to make the gradient too steep for both ascent and descent. In the case of the latter, the ability of a locomotive or locomotives to hold the train on the incline without skating is very important.

climb from the lower to the upper deck, most of it hidden. I quickly realized that, with a clear deck separation of 18in at a steady climb of 2 per cent, a linear run of 75ft would be required. A 2 per cent incline means that the line climbs 2in for every 100in of main line. This could be accommodated with some clever layout design; one method would be to do what the real railroads do and insert extended loops to gain altitude, hiding them in tunnels to disguise the fact that the train passes through the same scene more or less twice. However, this does not suit my chosen prototype and would call for wider baseboards to accommodate my minimum radius curvature together with baseboards at least 36in wide, much wider than I was planning to build. This type of layout structure was contrary to my near shelf layout design and also did not fit the linear nature of the MRL 4th Subdivision main line.

I soon concluded that the best way to encapsulate that climb into a sensibly contained space would be to build a helix – a complex joinery project which would leave my main line more linear in keeping with the prototype and remove the inappropriate double use of scenes, no matter how much main line length this could add to the run, but keeping the main line sincere, as discussed in Chapter 3. The deck separation within the helix was calculated at 2.25in, enough room for the tallest rolling stock (double-stack trains and tri-level auto carriers), as determined at the practical planning stage of the layout. I allowed for track and finger space too. Don't forget the thickness of the plywood used in each deck in the determination of deck separation.

This introduces another set of factors: the smaller the deck separation in the helix for each turn results in a smaller gradient for a given radius, although the limit is still the loading gauge for your models. However, to climb a given height within a helix you need more turns and therefore more timber, track and time to build it. The greater the helix deck separation, the fewer turns but the greater the gradient, which will impact on train performance.

The gradient is also affected by the radius of the helix: the greater the radius, the smaller the gradient for trains to tackle. This is set against an increased length of line for a given helix deck separation. For example,

my 16.25in radius over a 2.25in separation gave me the ruling 2.2 per cent incline, well within the capability of twelve or eighteen powered axles for an 11ft train. A 16.25in radius equates to 102in of line per turn. The result is the 2.2 per cent incline I calculated at the outset, and against which I ran tests with my locomotives. If the radius were 20in instead, that would equate to 125in of line per turn. Rising 2.25in over 125in gives an incline of 1.8 per cent, at the cost of a larger footprint of the helix and more track.

And that's the crux; the 'given' is the space between the helix decks as determined by the envelope of your rolling stock plus room for track and underlay – a measurement that is non-negotiable. The rest is a balance between a practicable gradient, a workable track radius and the footprint of the helix. Remember that your trains have a vote on this issue, so run some tests before settling on a set of dimensions.

There are many methods of building a helix, including the use of threaded rods or a core of hardboard curved to the correct radius. I chose a stacked helix separated by wooden riser blocks to keep things simple. For the record, a helix can be left as an un-scenic feature or enclosed in a mountain or something similar. Offsetting the decks also means that scenery can be introduced to the running line and even passing loops added, although the inner radius should not be less than your minimum for the layout as a whole. Staged loops and lapped loops can be incorporated in the helix to provide additional passing places and more train storage. Finally, while my helix links two decks with a single line, they can host two or more running lines, be bidirectional and link three or more decks. One thing was for sure though, this project was going to test my rudimentary joinery skills to their limits!

CALCULATIONS

Data: deck separation: 2.25in, track radius: 16.25in.

To calculate the length of running line in each turn: $2\pi r$ or $2 \times 3.14 \times 16.25 = 102$in.

The gradient of my helix is 2.25in divided by 102in to give an incline of 2.2 per cent. To reduce this to 2 per cent, for example, the main line run per turn would have to be 125in in length to rise 2.25in per turn. This would increase the area of the helix and the radius of track in each turn to nearly 20in.

To calculate the area covered by the helix, use πr^2, which in the case of my helix is 3.14×16.25^2. This gave me an area of the circle of 829sq.in or 6.7sq.ft. This was an acceptable use of space in my design, but any larger and I would be reconsidering my options for an N scale layout.

If working in larger scales with greater minimum radii of curves and a greater deck separation to accommodate taller stock, the helix is, logically, going to occupy much more space.

CUTTING WOOD ...

Quarter-turn segments 4in wide were cut from 9mm plywood by the hard method: a jigsaw – the 4in width being determined by the space needed for the track, the overhang of my longest items of rolling stock and the support blocks. Each one was carefully rid of splinters and rough edges before being placed in the order as they would be used on the helix to check whether they were reasonably accurate. After calculating the deck separation within the helix, allowing for the 9mm ply decks, I set up a power mitre saw to cut numerous riser

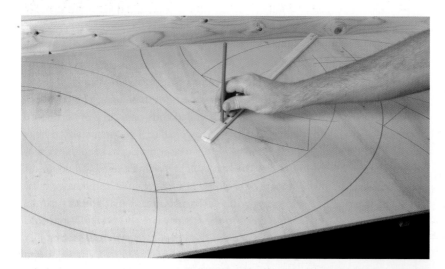

A simple wooden trammel was used to draw out the 90-degree helix deck segments on a large sheet of 9mm plywood; 9mm plywood was seen as desirable to keep to the minimum required deck separation.

Each segment was carefully cut by using a powered jigsaw – the job being completed out of doors because of the mess.

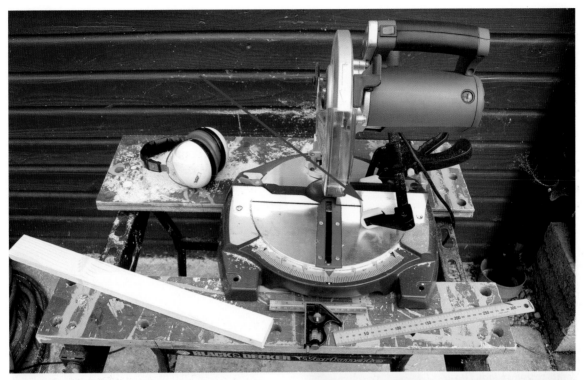

The helix decks are separated by riser blocks of 2in × 1in planed timber. Each one had to be cut very precisely indeed and over a hundred of them were required. They were sawn on a powered mitre saw like this one. The blue arrow shows a block clamped to the plate of the saw so that they could be cut quickly without my having to measure each one.

RIGHT: Setting up the saw was critical in the cutting of the blocks, so this view should further help in visualizing how it was done, should you wish to attempt the same construction design.

blocks as accurately as possible, which would be used to support each deck as the helix was constructed. A combination square was used to check the accuracy of each block, and those even slightly out were reject-ed. I made slightly different risers for the first turn of the helix which was to be supported on the L-girder baseboard frames. They were designed to be secured to the baseboard with clamps so that the incline could be accurately determined before I committed to a more permanent fixing (screws only at that stage, just in case adjustments were needed further down the line).

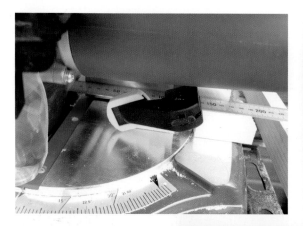

ABOVE: *The position of the block of wood used to make the stop against which my planed timber was pushed before cutting was very carefully measured.*

ABOVE RIGHT: *Each block was checked with a combination square. Those even slightly adrift were rejected. There is little or no room for joinery and measuring errors in the building of a helix.*

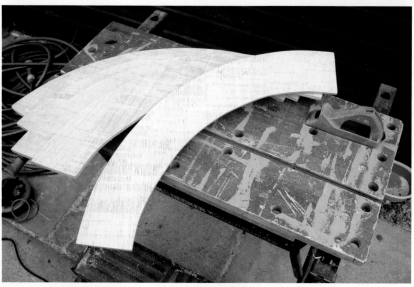

ABOVE: *Segments have to be carefully finished too, so that they can be handled without the risk of splinters.*

LEFT: *Each one was first profiled to as smooth a curve as possible with a rasp plane.*

*LEFT: **Wear gloves to save the hands from injury.***

*BELOW: **Glass paper finishes off each segment to a nice smooth edge.***

SETTING OUT THE HELIX

The precise position of the helix on the baseboard was set out by using a trammel as a guide. The position was adjusted to allow for a single running line which passes around the back of the helix. Once the first four segments were placed on the baseboard, the first risers could be positioned and their locations checked to see that adequate support would result. I discovered that two additional joists were needed for attaching the first risers. I also wished to keep the middle of the helix clear of obstruction for access. This setting out exercise is key to getting the incline precise, and throughout the seven-turn climb there could be no variation in the climb within the helix as there is little room for error at this stage. The measuring and positioning of the risers took several hours, but I knew that once this was right, I could pile the rest on top relatively quickly. Each riser was fixed to the segments that would form the first turn, and they were in turn clamped to the baseboard joists. Each one was adjusted with the aid of clamps before being screwed in place. For the record, the first riser has to be at the 90-degree position and that should be 25 per cent of the deck separation measurement. The 180-degree riser has to be at 50 per cent of the separation measurement, and so on until you achieve the first full turn immediately over 'ground zero', which should be supported by riser blocks of the full deck separation in size.

Track was placed on the helix and a test run undertaken with a train that happened to be to hand, to see whether the first turn was as even as I had hoped. Adjustments were made to level the deck across its width by using a Torpedo spirit level at each riser as well as checking the gradient. Screws were driven into the risers to secure them to the joists.

After that, it was simply a case of building each turn on to what I hoped was a solid foundation. The track (Atlas code 55 set track curves at 16.25in radius) was placed and secured on each deck before the next turn was built up until the summit was reached. The test train was run after every turn had been completed to check for errors or uneven track laying. When the 18in of altitude was reached, a lead off piece was built so the track would lead away on to the upper deck. The final altitude of the running line is 19in above the lower deck ground zero point after the lead off was established.

You may be wondering why the helix was constructed before the second deck was started. The reason is simple: the final height of the top deck of the helix at the desired lead off point to turn the main line in the desired direction would determine the exact height of the top deck of the layout. To build the latter first and then get the helix to fit might have introduced an unwanted complication if measurements were off the mark by even a small amount. Bear in mind that the top deck of the helix cannot level off unless it is offset from the deck below by the required clearances for the tallest rolling stock or the separation and therefore the clearance in the final turn of the helix would be reduced and might prove unworkable. To change the gradient to reach the surface of the upper level suddenly would also introduce a sharpening of the climb at the point when ascending trains least needed it. I wanted to stick to my maximum gradient of 2.2 per cent for the whole layout, knowing that the performance of the locomotives would be more than equal to it.

Wiring was next, and the use of set track segments, while making track laying simple, was going to make the use of droppers for each length of running rail a big job. As the layout is being built for DCC control, I ran a pair of red and black 24/0.2 cables up the inside of one leg of the helix with enough slack to connect to the main power bus run. Red and black, the usual convention, was used. The feed droppers to the track consisted of single-strand bell wire. Every effort was made to keep the wiring as simple and neat as possible.

That concludes the story of my helix and why I chose to spend many hours building one. The benefits for my layout were clear: an additional 100ft of main line in which I can hide long trains to extend the run on the layout or use as on-line staging. It's a talking point for visitors and also links the two decks of the layout with an efficient (if non-prototypical) structure. A helix has to be carefully considered to match the various factors one faces in layout design, such as the performance of locomotives, their ability both to climb a stiff gradient and brake a heavy train running back down without skating on the rails, gauge, available space and how it can be fitted into the overall scheme.

While my chosen scheme is based on Montana mountain railroading, it does not mean that the use of a helix is exclusive to US-model railroading practice. Modellers from anywhere, no matter the company they are modelling, can take advantage of a helix to get more out of their available space. After all, space in the railway room is not only horizontal but vertical too. If a joinery exercise like this is not to your taste, then a commercial helix kit may provide the answer. For me, this one opened up a host of exciting design possibilities and an amazingly long main line run!

This picture shows the large, square, L-girder frame which was built to support the helix. Additional joists are likely to be required and their position is determined as the helix is laid out on the frame.

The first four segments are placed at 'ground zero' so the position of the first risers could be determined. This exercise also helped to determine where additional joists were needed to support the first turn of the helix.

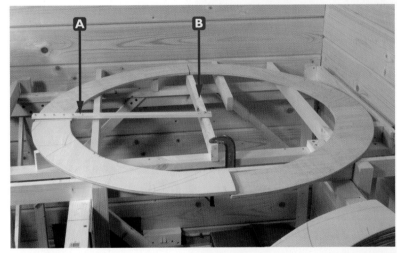

A trammel (A) fitted to a temporary joist (B) was used to assess the exact position of the helix decks and ultimately, the centre line for the track itself.

A closer view of the finished segments and the trammel.

The additional joists were fitted to the L-girder frame before work started on the critical first turn of the helix.

It never hurts to spend time on a dry run just to see how it is likely to shape up. Make any necessary changes at this stage, not after assembly has started.

The first risers were screwed and glued to the first four deck segments before being clamped to the joists at ground zero. The risers for the first turn consisted of pieces of 9mm plywood.

The process of establishing the gradient is now undertaken and accuracy is vital – take your time over this – it took me several hours to complete this task. Every measurement was checked many times and the gradient was checked with a simple tool made from an engineer's square, a Torpedo spirit level and a piece of wood with simple graduations on it. Get it wrong and the error will work into every turn of the helix.

ABOVE: Level each deck across its width as you set the incline. A Torpedo sprit level is a useful tool for this job.

RIGHT: Clamping each riser and segment subassembly to the joists before committing to a more permanent fixing allows for adjustments to be made to the gradient.

The first turn is shown complete, with the first circle of track in place. Place the track at every turn – it is easier than fitting track when the whole structure is complete.

An interesting detail is this method of securing the first four segments together. As the helix rises, the riser blocks will take on this role.

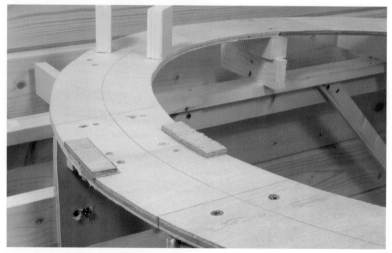

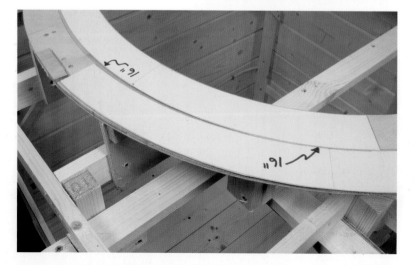

Cardboard templates are used repeatedly to check the radius of the helix, together with the centre line for the track because the trammel can no longer be used for this task as the helix rises.

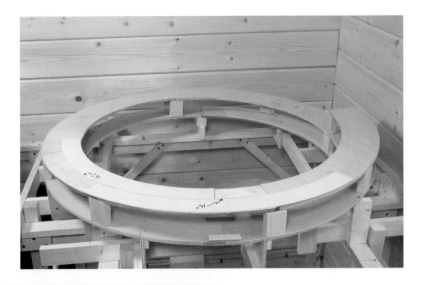

The second turn deck of the helix is dry-run fitted to check for accuracy. Note the use of curved templates cut from mounting card.

A side view of the second test assembly of the second turn.

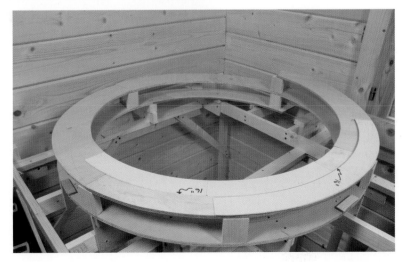

This view shows the risers and blocks used to achieve the second turn of the helix.

Use set track instead of flexible track in a helix so that precise curvature can be easily achieved.

Track is laid temporarily on the first turn and the clearances between riser blocks are checked with the longest item of rolling stock in the collection. It is better to fix errors at this stage rather than later.

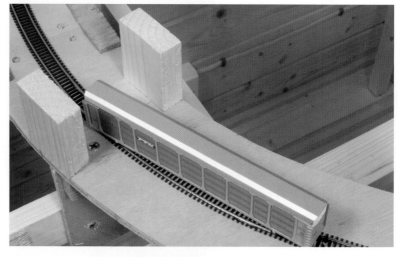

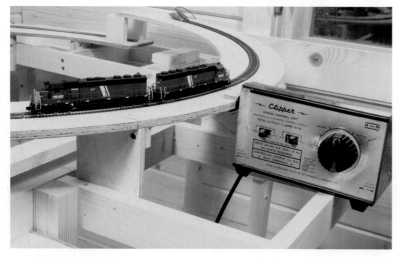

Once you are happy with the lower deck and the clearances, the first circle of track is installed and tested. A pair of Inter-Mountain SD45-2 locomotives in Montana Rail Link colours just happened to be to hand for this job.

Enter the hot glue gun, which will help to speed up construction. Hot glue makes a great 'permanent' clamp allowing other glues to set in their due time.

White wood glue is applied to the point where the riser block is to be attached. Don't fit the block just yet!

A blob or two of hot glue is applied to the riser block before the riser block is quickly pressed into place. The hot glue holds the block in place, like a clamp, allowing the white glue to form a strong bond undisturbed while construction continues.

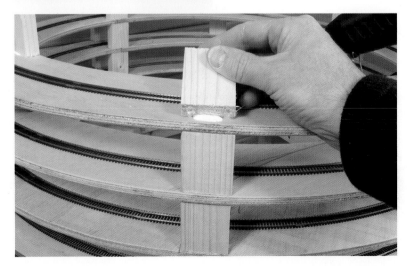

With all measurements established and double checked, the helix just builds up, turn after turn. Each is checked before continuing construction. The track should sit exactly above itself on each successive turn.

Lay the track on each turn as it is built because placing track in a completed helix is a nightmare. Set track simplified construction considerably and was more uniform than flexible track in this type of structure.

The riser blocks are located, as far as possible, on top of each other and additional ones are added along the outer edge of the decks for stability. It is not possible to drive screws from the underside, as you can see – hence the use of the white glue and hot glue technique. The deck segments can be screwed and glued into the top of the risers though.

This picture shows how a lead off segment (at 19in height from ground zero in the case of my helix) is fitted. Note that it is on a gradient to prevent the loading gauge clearance on the last turn of the helix from being compromised.

Wiring up for Digital Command Control – the main feed from the power bus comprises red and black 24/0.2 cables run up the side of the helix and feeds to each turn were installed using bell wire. The down side of set track is all those rail joiners which could be problematic in the future. Note the connection to the second deck of the layout, the lead-off being changed to suit a slight change in the design.

Remember, the trains always have a vote in everything you do and if this large, thirty-car coal drag found it difficult to use the helix, then all that work would have been for nothing. However, spending time testing the capability of locomotives on inclines together with careful measurement, setting out and testing has resulted in a successful project.

CHAPTER EIGHT

MULTI-DECK CONSTRUCTION TECHNIQUES

Multi-deck layouts take full advantage of the volume of a room as well as its footprint. You can accommodate a great deal more railway for your given area. This picture shows the top deck of my concept, with the helix joining the lower and the middle deck visible in the background.

INTRODUCTION

How can you get more bangs for your bucks with layout design? Go for two or more decks and extend the length of your main line or branch line to run longer trains or to accommodate a second or even a third layout theme in the same room. I was fortunate enough to choose an out-building with high ceilings, making a three-tier layout a possibility, complete with a people underpass under the third deck for access to all the operating aisle space.

Building a second deck to any layout is little different from putting up shelves for books or similar such modifications. The same can be said for the third deck too. OK, it becomes necessary to make adjustments to accommodate risers to support the sub-road bed and track bed as well as the operational equipment such as stationary decoders, turnout machines and wiring. You have to consider how they are to be linked, either by a helix, a mechanical device or by simply building the layout on a gentle gradient around the wall of the room. By the time the baseboard construction reaches the starting point, your layout should have a deck 12 or more inches above the lower baseboards. This design is called a 'mushroom layout', and some modellers will build up the floor in areas to match the gain in elevation of the rail. However, a continual, graded layout will need 600in of track to rise 12in in height, which equates to 50ft of running length. Do you have a large enough room to accommodate such a design? There are tricks and techniques to achieve this, including single-turn helices hidden in tunnels or behind buildings, trees and rock outcrops.

When going for the double or multi-deck approach, you are, in effect, building a layout concept within a concept: a shelf layout over the main bottom deck baseboards. How they are linked on my project was covered in the last chapter, which looked at the building of a helix; not the simplest of structures to complete, certainly not the most authentic, but a very useful layout planning and design tool nonetheless.

A visit to a home improvement store quickly reveals a lot of shelving options that could be adapted for layout construction. In the design of my second and third deck, I tried several systems for creating the deck shelves. I also continued the practice of using girders and joists for the main sub-road bed support structure, as it had proved to be so successful on the round-the-walls part of the bottom deck. The change I made to the L-girder construction method was to build them on the shelves as I went along, rather than on the floor. I limited the width of the middle and the upper deck to 22in – any more and I think stability would have become a problem.

The techniques demonstrated in this chapter could also be used to create a single-deck shelf layout, attached to the walls of a room, so, if a multi-deck layout is not your thing, give consideration to the techniques described here to create narrow, space-saving, shelf designs which may work out as a better option for your space and theme.

CONSIDERATIONS

The separation or space between decks is an important layout design consideration, which was discussed in Chapter 3 under layout design. Will you have enough room for large layout design elements, such as grain elevators? It is important to leave sufficient space between the top of one deck and the underside of the second so that you can view straight into the back of the scene. A second deck does not need as much separation as it is always going to be further from the floor and more likely to be closer to eye level. I gave consideration to how the deck separation distances are influenced by the depth of the decks themselves. My second and third deck are 5in from the underside of the girders to the top of the joists and sub-road bed, assuming the latter is not on risers. I also gave thought to the size of my preferred turnout machine, the Circuitron 'Tortoise', which is 100mm deep, requiring at least 4in of depth to the frames to conceal both the motor and wiring. Another important layout feature that benefits from a second and a third deck is lighting – allow for a method of attaching layout lighting to the underside of the decks, and, when

choosing it, remember that the distance from the light source to the model is quite small.

Here are some points you should think about when looking at a second or a third deck:

- Are the walls of your layout room strong enough to support such a structure? Stud and dry walling is notoriously difficult for assembling shelving at the best of times. Buy a stud locator, find out where the wooden timber strips that support the dry wall lining are positioned behind the dry wall lining and use them as a secure fixing point to support metal shelf brackets.
- If building a shelf layout in a wooden building, check that the walls are stable enough. My building is composed of 80mm machined logs that do not flex. However, I had to be sure that the building had settled before starting work on the decks.
- Secure your shelf layout on separate timber upright members attached direct to the walls if you can. They will provide a frame for the back drop and are easier to fix to the wall, using shims of wood to ensure that they are 100 per cent vertical and level in all planes. After all, your walls may not be totally flat. A useful material to use is dry wall studding which is usually very stable, smooth and strong. It can be bought in 2.4m lengths.
- Consider how wiring and other equipment is to be concealed underneath a second and a third deck so that it does not impact on the layout deck below.
- Look into the placing of controls for a second deck and how they relate to control points on the lower decks. This is important to ensure that there are no congestion points when the layout is in use.
- Throttle plug in points for the control of trains do not necessarily need to be placed in the fascia of the second and subsequent decks.
- Lighting fixtures are important considerations, especially as the second deck will shadow the one below.

- If stability proves to be a problem, consider using threaded rods to partly suspend a deck from the ceiling.
- Buy the strongest shelf brackets you can afford and be prepared to supplement them with metal angles.
- If you are planning to use a helix, build that structure first before commencing on the upper deck as the height of the track bed at the top of the helix will ultimately determine the precise height of the second and subsequent decks.
- Layout design elements, such as big trestle bridges, which, by their very nature, cross deep river channels with lots of great scenic features such as rock formations, may present a challenge in the design of the layout. If your channel cuts 12in down below the track bed, how will this affect the scenery on the deck below? It will have to be positioned over an off-stage area where the reduced headroom on the deck below will be of no concern.
- How strong is your lower deck bench work frame? Could you stand on it with your full weight to help with work such as track laying on the second deck? Now that's an interesting thought.

WHAT WILL A DECK SUPPORT?

Check the maximum loading of metal shelving brackets and the wall fixings you plan to use very carefully. Although most of a shelf layout will not have too much weight on it, I had to look seriously at the weight of rock castings for the second deck of my MRL N scale plan and the third deck area, which would support the 'Dover' staging yard of the Folkestone East layout. It would not take that many 500g OO gauge locomotives such as the Heljan Class 47 or the Bachmann Class 66 to result in a considerable loading of those shelves. Like most modellers, I do like collecting large locomotives.

BUILDING THE SECOND DECK

I decided upon a common format of metal shelving brackets, from my local home improvement store, screwed to dry wall framing timber, itself screwed to the walls and spaced roughly 34in apart. A piece of 4in × 1in planed wood was screwed to the brackets to form a secure foundation to which the long girders could be screwed. Once they were in place, the joists could be fitted, spaced approximately 11in apart, but

This is the appearance of a multi-deck layout showing the various structural elements, including the uprights screwed to the wall to provide a completely solid and vertical support for the shelves.

Look for metal angle brackets like these at your local hardware store. They are very useful for stabilizing the deck shelves.

not glued in case one needed to be moved to accommodate a turnout machine or other device.

A spirit level and a long piece of straight wood were a simple but essential combination to have to hand to check the level of each bracket in relation to the next, so that the resulting shelf was level from end to end. The ends of the deck were fixed to the walls, providing much needed support.

In the event, I decided that my choice of shelving bracket would not ensure total stability, so the joists at each bracket were removed and fitted with steel angle plates to provide further rigidity. The joist was refitted, with one leg of the bracket screwed to the upright member. The result was a considerable improvement in stability – lesson learned – don't go cheap on brackets.

My short Torpedo spirit level was found to be invaluable once again, being used to check the level of the shelf across its width, which seems to be its primary purpose, and adjustments were made as required. At all times, anything present on the lower deck was covered with a protective sheet to prevent damage. I had started to place track on the lower deck to get something running, and, on reflection, I should have been more patient and started work only after the main structure of the second deck was complete.

This type of angle bracket was added to my second deck after I had determined that the shelving brackets were not strong enough on their own. The third deck did not have shelving brackets, requiring only steel angle plates for support. The ends of the baseboards were attached to the walls, which meant that support was required only in the middle.

My initial choice was to use this type of economical metal shelving bracket. On reflection, I did wonder how it would cope with the weight of the shelf structure and the load of rock castings required to create Montanan mountain scenery.

Levels are important – all the brackets had to be at the same height from the deck level below. The 4in × 1in planed wood provided a mount to which the long girders could be attached.

Looking the other way: shelf layouts are ideal for round-the-walls locations like this. The peninsula built into the middle of the room required a slightly different approach.

The long girders are composed of 2in × 2in planed timber. This view from the underside shows the long girders in place and the joists of 2in × 1in timber at right angles to the long girders.

Each joist fitted over the shelving brackets is fitted with a steel angle plate for additional rigidity.

A view of the long girders during construction. The N scale models seen in this shot offer a perspective on the additional space and running length that the shelf layout and second deck concepts offer layout designers.

A view showing how the second deck relates to and impacts on the lower deck. The track and control equipment are in place at this eastern end of the line being modelled. The reverse loop helps in restaging trains after an operating session and for access to the storage roads to the rear of the baseboard.

Holes are drilled through the joists to accommodate equipment wire for turnout motors and the DCC power bus wires. This simple technique does not weaken the joists and ensures that they will not hang down over the deck below.

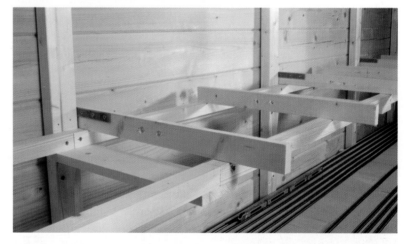

INSTALLING THE SUB-ROAD OR TRACK BED

Two types of sub-road bed were to be used on the second deck, which would, in the main, support single- and double-track running lines. The long straights to the rear of the second deck which are off-stage sections of line with no scenery, were constructed from 12mm plywood. The scenic sections of line would be constructed by using spline sub-road bed, a technique described in Chapter 9.

The plywood sections, which were cut to a length to coincide with the joists so that the joins would be over a riser for a more secure fixing, were to be fixed to simple risers of 2in × 1in timber, plywood off-cuts or any other timber off-cuts left over from the construction process. Each may be fitted to the plywood sections to expedite levelling work or left loose until the risers were finally screwed to the shelf joists.

The height of the sub-road bed over the joists was carefully measured and the risers clamped to the joists. Either a spirit level or a simple gradient device was attached to the plywood and the plywood strips adjusted to the correct gradient or levels. A Torpedo spirit level further showed its value in being used to check levels across the width of the sub-road bed before the clamps were finally tightened and screws driven into the risers to secure them to the joists.

This levelling technique is applicable to sub-road bed construction using spines too. After all, the process of achieving a correctly levelled sub-road bed or a smooth incline and transition from level to gradient is the same regardless of the sub-road bed construction method.

 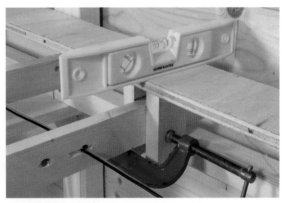

ABOVE: Risers consisting of blocks of wood are fitted to the shelf joists and are clamped into place. The sub-road bed, consisting of plywood in this case, is levelled by adjusting the position of each riser. The risers may be fitted to the plywood to assist with this technique, if required.

ABOVE RIGHT: A Torpedo spirit level indicates how level the width of the sub-road bed is. Note that the DCC power bus wires have already been installed.

LEFT: The corner location of the room was a bit tricky to complete and required more than the usual care in levelling to prevent any unwanted camber.

Each length of plywood was cut to length to coincide with the risers and joists to provide a firm location for screw fixings. Note the care taken to countersink the pilot hole so that the screws do not cause a lump in the cork track bed when it is laid.

Levelling at each stage of this process is vital so that the track bed remains level across its width, even on gradients. This long, straight section of line is an off-stage or hidden line (but accessible in case of accidents) which ruins the length of the upper deck to get the line back to the right end of the deck, so a constant east–west alignment of the railway is achieved for operational integrity.

Clamping a spirit level to each board when checking levels along the length of the sub-road bed will do much to avoid errors and to keep the plywood sub-road bed straight.

A side view of the all-important levelling process, showing the risers attached to the joists using clamps.

The length of joists can be adapted to suit the location. The longer joists at the eastern end of the second deck are designed to support a turn-back loop, bringing the off-stage line along the back of the deck round to the front and therefore on-stage onto the scenic part of the layout once again.

Another view of the second deck in relation to the bottom deck. This part of the lower deck will be scenic and represents the arrival and departure roads of West Missoula. The line curves away to the west to West Missoula Junction and then on toward the helix and DesMet Junction.

The second deck meets the helix with a gentle 1.5 per cent incline, which was designed into the layout at the top of the helix to avoid another turn of the helix itself. In the event, that last climb off the helix was too much for some locomotives and it was removed in favour of another helix deck, which was retrospectively added a few weeks after this picture was taken.

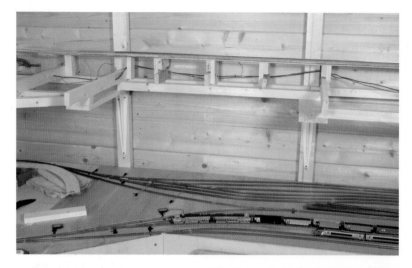

This alarming gap in the second deck is to accommodate a steel trestle. This is to be bridge 165, at milepost 165, also known as Fish Creek, an important layout design element of the prototype 4th Sub line on the Montana Rail Link, which is a signature structure and had to be included.

The trestle bridge location was carefully planned so that the drop section of the second deck to be built here would be over an off-stage area of the lower deck, and therefore should have no impact on the scenery or structures on the lower deck. The scenic part of the lower deck commences just beyond this point with a curved back drop and a highway bridge over the yard.

Work on the third deck began with calculating the height of the 'nod-under' or people access underpass. This is a balance between the height of the rail of the second deck and not making the nod-under too low or reducing the deck separation between the middle and the top deck by too much so that the scenery would be unacceptably compressed.

No shelving brackets were used to support the top deck, and the long girders were composed of L-girder built using 3in × 1in planed wood, with a 2in × 1in flange for strength. The joists were of the same 2in × 1in planed timber as before.

Although the top deck section along the walls of the building is shown here, the deck top was still to be fitted. That was intended to be of 12mm plywood. This section of the top deck will support the main line and one staging yard for Folkestone East, together with the staging yard for the planned US outline HO scale layout when it is started.

ON TO THE NEXT TASKS

With the round-the-walls section of the layout complete with its second deck, frames for the third deck in place and a good connection between the second deck and the helix established, it was time to complete the heavy duty bench work construction by building the free-standing peninsula, the structure that would occupy the middle of the room.

This would enable me to complete the second and the third deck joinery, including the access people underpass. With the peninsula in place, phase 1 of the MRL main line could be finished, wired up and made operational, leaving the second deck track road sub bed, track, wiring and operational equipment to be completed as phase 2 at a later date.

The layouts intended for the third or top deck will be looked into in more detail once the peninsula is completed; with the first phase of the British EM gauge layout, Folkestone East started using ready-to-place flexi track and turnouts completed by using kits which were made up on the work bench well in advance of the building of the third deck. Progress to a fully operational main line and staging yards could be made quite quickly. The third layout theme is a little way off, even at this stage of construction, because much research remained to be done on the layout theme that will occupy the space on the opposite side of the double-sided peninsula. So, the peninsula is an important part of the layout design and, when finished, will open up all sorts of possibilities.

CHAPTER NINE

BUILDING THE PENINSULA

With the top deck in place, forming the final level of the triple deck concept, the fun task of placing trains on the sub-road bed to visualize how the plan will fit, could begin.

INTRODUCTION

Key to the construction of an oval layout plan on a third deck, together with extending the N scale MRL main line on the lower and the middle deck, was the construction of a peninsula. This is a free-standing structure that extends across the middle of the layout cabin, ending 24in from the wall baseboards on the opposite side and creating a walk-through aisle to access what would become an inner aisle. If you recall the discussion regarding layout height in Chapter 3, the decision on the height of the third deck had to be a balance between being able to work on it comfortably, being able to enjoy the trains without teetering on the top of a big stepladder, having sufficient head room for scenery between the top deck and the ceiling and, most importantly, being high enough for a people under-pass giving comfortable access to the middle aisle.

A peninsula baseboard can be double-sided too, with scenery on both sides of a double-skinned back drop on any decks constructed on it, so do give that

planning point some consideration. In the case of my double-sided peninsula, the MRL main line can run along one side, around the end of the peninsula and back along the opposite side, extending the length of the main line, introducing additional loops and creating two separate scenes, which are not visible from each other. It's a technique commonly used in layout planning by modellers in North America and the objective is to make the line appear longer than it is, together with the illusion of the train 'going somewhere'.

On the top deck, which bridges the aisle through to the middle operating area, the double-sided design enabled me to consider two layout themes: one can occupy the space facing the front, with a second, smaller plan, placed on the opposite side. On a circular layout, the tracks for both layouts (and they may be of different scale and gauge) may occupy the same baseboards used for staging. Back scenes will visually and scenically separate the two layouts, so each operator will not be distracted by the other.

One of the signature trains for the Folkestone East theme is a Travelling Post Office or TPO. The models allocated to the formation of the South-East TPO are placed on the layout to help in transferring the track plan to the baseboards.

Peninsulas may also be built at an angle across the room to further extend the running length of main lines, but be aware of the effect that this will have on curves and the possible creation of aisle pinch points which could become irritating bottlenecks for your operating crew to negotiate while trying to concentrate on running trains.

My peninsula was built at right angles from the wall, with a turn back 'blob' on the end to allow wide-radius curves on the N scale MRL layout. This prevented too much of a bottleneck through the access nod-under or underpass. Furthermore, the shape better suited the design for the top deck layouts, enabling a continuous oval track plan for Folkestone East to be employed for test running together with end-to-end running for prototypical operation.

BOX FRAME CONSTRUCTION AND THE DOMINO CONCEPT

I chose box frame construction for this vital, free-standing structure. The boxes are made up as equally sized, modular units before being assembled into the desired peninsula shape. Each box frame is 40in × 24in in size, constructed from 4in × 1in planed timber. Remember, with stability an important factor, choose timber that is not warped, cupped, dished or twisted when planning box frame construction. The boxes were both screwed and glued together using a picture framing square to aid building before the completed frames were assembled into the desired layout shape.

This technique introduces the idea and principles of modular construction once again but from a slightly different angle. Many modellers create box frames to set dimensions and exacting standards using planed timber or strips of 12mm and 18mm plywood. In having set dimensions, they can be assembled in any format: end-to-end, side-to-side, end-to side and so on, to suit any layout format. Sometimes, these layouts are temporary, with the box frames bolted together with big M10 nuts, bolts and washers so that they are easily uncoupled from each other and moved around to a new format. The baseboard tops or sub-road bed and track layouts are temporary, being lifted and replaced when the new format has been decided upon.

It's a form of portable layout construction without the complexity of having a completely portable layout which never changes format but is assembled in the same way time after time. Domino construction, as this system is commonly called, offers greater flexibility to the modeller, providing the means to try something different every few years without the expensive ripping up of scenery and track, which would be the case with a more permanent, fixed layout concept. Builders of domino layouts frequently loose-lay track on top of the sub-road bed, ignore powered turnouts in favour of manual ground throws and detail scenes to a minimalist standard so that the right atmosphere is created for authentic operation. Cost is kept to a minimum.

An extreme example of domino construction is in the use of flat-surfaced, hollow-core doors. Perfect as ready made baseboards and easily purchased from a home improvement store, they are generally stable and strong enough for layout construction. Extruded insulation foam may be used on top of hollow-core doors so a landscape may be introduced to the model. The door concept has several benefits: they are all the same size and shape, they are strong and they are most certainly cheap. It's a concept that has been used to save countless modellers time and money.

Given that my peninsula project is not likely to be dismantled to create a different layout format, each box frame was screwed rather than bolted together, with gusset plates on the outside of each join for further strength. I wanted the whole assembly to be strong enough to support my weight, should I need to stand on the frames when building the middle and upper decks. That's before I start work on track and scenery, of course.

FITTING THE LEGS

Legs are composed of 2in × 2in planed timber, fitted to the inside corners of the box frames and at those joins in the box frames where uprights for the middle and the upper deck will be secured. The legs also provide bracing for the upright members and so had to be fitted in the same line. As the box frames were assembled together away from the wall, temporary legs were clamped to the leading edge of the peninsula construction while levelling was undertaken. The permanent legs were then simply screwed in place and the temporary ones removed until the next pair of frames were bolted in place.

DECK CONSTRUCTION

I chose to use the hefty planed timber sold as dry wall studding. I prefer it because it is usually very stable,

straight and smooth. Hefty enough to support the decks and tall enough when sold in 2.4m lengths to be able to accommodate two decks. A cross member or joist was fitted at 90 degrees to each upright for the second deck, after careful measurement from the floor to achieve the correct height and levels. For the long sections linking the joists, I resorted to L-girders, attaching them to the joists first rather than building them off the layout and adding them later. On top of the L-girders were fitted more joists of 2in × 1in planed timber. These would support the risers and sub-road bed.

The third deck was built in much the same way, with joists screwed to the uprights, supporting L-girders and joists to support the sub-road bed. Fascia boards were added to the ends of the joists to provide a smooth finish to the baseboards on the middle and the upper deck. I found that 3in × 1in timber was perfect for this job, and the use of 2.4m lengths further stabilized and strengthened the peninsula decks. Each deck was fixed to the outer walls for further stability.

PEOPLE UNDERPASS

My personal experience of 'duck-under' access points to reach central operating areas is one of bumped heads, crawling on the floor and discomfort. I was determined to avoid a duck-under, but to achieve a sensibly designed top deck concept, I decided that a nod-under would be more acceptable. This was built into the layout to allow access to the middle aisle created by the building of the peninsula. L-girders formed the main structure of the span, which was fixed to one exterior wall. The underside of the access nod-under is lined with hardboard, which helps to prevent injury should one forget to keep one's head down when passing through and to prevent any wiring runs from hanging down and strangling the unwary. When considering such an access point, discuss the height and the width with your operating crew to ensure that it will not cause problems. Be sure that your team is comfortable with your plans, for the sake of an inch or two in height.

The following sequence of photographs demonstrates how the peninsula was constructed.

Frames of box construction are built one at a time to predetermined dimensions so that they will bolt or screw together. This is also referred to as 'domino' construction because the frames go together like dominoes. Note the large clamps holding the frames together ready for screw assembly.

BELOW: Square off the box frame assemblies carefully with a picture-framing square. Anything out of true will cause problems later when the frames are assembled to form the layout structure.

LEFT: A combined drill and countersink bit is used to drill accurate pilot holes for screw assembly. Glue is also used on each joint for strength.

ABOVE: Care is taken to ensure that each bracing piece fitted across the frame is square and true. After all, they will be used to hold risers for the bottom deck railway and the long uprights needed to support the middle and the upper deck.

LEFT: The box frames are placed together to suit the design of the baseboards, in this case, my peninsula. They were arranged side to side, like dominoes, and screwed together. Legs with bracing are clamped in place while levels are determined both across the frame and along its length.

Work is progressing well – it's amazing how quickly this type of construction can proceed with even the simplest of tools and a little patience. The ugly front of the frames will be covered with a smooth, curved and painted fascia when all the construction of the frames, decks and track sub bed has been completed.

ABOVE: *Simple gusset plates strengthen each join on the peninsula structure. The base structure appears to be overly engineered for the task of holding a simple, single-track main line. However, to expedite construction on the top deck, the frame had to take my full weight so that I could work on the top deck framing, as well as provide a stable base for the decks.*

RIGHT: *Another view of the leg arrangement and the bracing used to stabilize the free-standing peninsula.*

BELOW: *The end of the peninsula has a 'blob' to enable a wide radius turn back on the main line. Note the access aisle between the peninsula and the far baseboard that allows walk round or roaming operation of the N scale MRL layout.*

The corners are angled to ease access through this potential pinch point for the movement of operators around the layout. When the fascia is fitted, the angles will be rounded off. Also worthy of note is that part of the end frame overhangs by about 18in. This makes it easier to move storage boxes through the gap by sliding them along the floor.

There are a lot of screws used in this construction – around 1,200 for the peninsula alone. No glue is used to join the box frames to each other just in case adjustments are necessary.

This photograph was taken from the central operating aisle towards the end of the peninsula to place it in perspective with the rest of the layout.

Uprights for the second and the top deck structure are composed both of 2in × 3in timber and dry wall framing timber 2.4m metres in length so that they rest on the floor. They are secured to the frames as shown in this photograph.

The uprights are braced under the baseboards with strips of planed timber attached to the legs. They are seen ready for attaching the main joists that will support L-girders for both the middle and the top deck.

The first joists are fitted at 90 degrees to the uprights and L-girder framing is added, one length of 2in × 1in at a time. Unlike the lower deck construction described in Chapter 6, the L-girders are assembled a piece at a time rather than being preassembled off the layout for addition later. Lengths are added very much where they are needed for strength as much as for any graceful design principle.

LEFT: Framing for the top deck is assembled in much the same manner, by making up the L-girders in situ. When calculating deck separation, allow for the depth of joists, L-girder framing and the track sub bed.

ABOVE: The top deck runs the full length of the room and across the access aisle, as seen in this picture. This creates the nod-under described in the main text, which has 66in of clearance between the floor and the underside of the L-girder.

BELOW: Those L-girders have sharp edges and will catch the unwary. When construction was completed, a sheet of hardboard was fitted to the underside to provide protection, and padding will do the rest.

Joists and frames are screwed into place. Never glue your joists just in case you need to move one. The ends of the joists are ugly but will be hidden by a smooth fascia when the layout moves on to the finishing and scenery stages. The ends of the joists will provide secure fixing points for the fascia boards. However, that is a little way off.

INSTALLING SUB-ROAD (TRACK) BED

Both the lower and the middle deck on the peninsula will support the MRL 4th Sub mainline through rural countryside, running alongside the Clark Fork River. The actual permanent way is relatively narrow, being a single track line with passing places. To create a gently curving main line and a good turn back curve at the end of the peninsula, I used spline sub-road bed construction rather than plywood sub-road bed. I soon established that cutting smooth flowing shapes and the easements or transition curves was going to be both wasteful and difficult to do accurately from plywood.

Spine road bed is constructed from thin lengths of wood or some other similar material such as homasote or particle board, which is glued together in a laminate structure for strength. The smooth flowing curvature essential for a curving main line in hill country was established by using one length of strip wood along the desired path of the track and a black marker pen to mark it on to the baseboard frames.

Screws are driven into the baseboard frames to provide a former, against which the spline track bed can be assembled until it is complete. Each spline has to be clamped to the temporary locating screw as each one is added – you need a lot of clamps for this

task. The spline assembly, either complete or part-complete, may then be screwed into place or lifted on to risers before being secured with screws. Experience has shown that material about 4mm thick is ideal for curves down to a 20in radius, ideal for my N scale layout. The use of thicker material means only that curves of larger radius will be possible, which will suit HO/OO and O gauge.

There are many advantages in using spline sub-road bed over plywood road bed. I discovered the following points as I planned and executed my first 20ft of spline road bed:

- The technique is flexible, producing gently curving road bed which helps create smoothly flowing track formations.
- Splines may be cut from almost any stable material, including fibre board materials and plywood.
- A great number of strips may be cut from a single sheet.
- The depth of the strips can be varied to suit the required location, strength and the length of span between supports.
- The structure of laminated splines is very strong and will have enough tensile strength to span long distances between risers.
- There is little waste.

● Strip wood of about 4 to 6mm width can be used very successfully provided that it has no knots or flaws that may weaken it.

● Track bed is constructed to be as wide as required; the greater depth of splines over plywood sub-road bed means that even thin track bed sections of only 1in width are possible, but without the numerous supporting risers.

There are some downsides to spline sub-road bed construction. The first one is the time taken to rip splines from sheet material. You have to be sure that each spline is absolutely straight and of a consistent width along its length, but I had neither the tools nor skill to achieve that. Ripping numerous lengths of particle board and plywood is messy, something I wished to avoid. Asking a timber supplier to do the ripping for you could be costly, and explaining to him exactly what you want together with the tiniest margins for error – well, I think you have the idea.

Spline sub-road bed takes some time to build, splines being laminated to the assembly one at a time and then clamped until the glue is completely hard before the next one is added. This is very important when you consider the forces the wood comes under, at least initially when it is used to create curves. As each spline is added, the curved sections become prestressed and take on the required shape, retaining it when the clamps are released. This means that the choice of glue is very

important for stable spline road bed, as is any additional support provided by driving screws into the side of the spines to strengthen the sub-road bed, especially on the sharper curves. I chose to use 4mm thick strip wood for my spline road bed, which was 1in in depth and purchased in lengths of 2.4m, which creates some good long runs of road bed. To save material, my laminates were built by using spacing blocks which were positioned over riser locations to begin with. I soon discovered that screws can be driven into the risers between the spines just as effectively.

The following sequence of photographs demonstrates how spine sub-road bed was constructed on the lower deck of the peninsula, and plywood sub-road bed for the top deck Folkestone East theme. The latter used plywood due to the yard scene which would be constructed on the scenic part of the layout. Using spline road bed for yards of more than two tracks and flat urban areas is not ideal, the technique being better suiting rural railway track. For the Folkestone East and the Missoula yard area of the MRL N scale layout well-supported plywood was more cost effective and quicker to install.

So what comes next? With the sub-road bed in place, the cork or foam road bed may be fitted and the track laid. Wiring and control systems come next. This is where the construction enters an exciting phase – the first run of any phase of a project is always an exciting – and worrying time. Will it work first time?

Sub-road bed is installed on the peninsula before fascias are added. I did not use spline sub-track or road bed on the upper deck Folkestone East layout, opting for 12mm ply, well supported with risers. This photograph shows the Kent coast mainline track bed being installed.

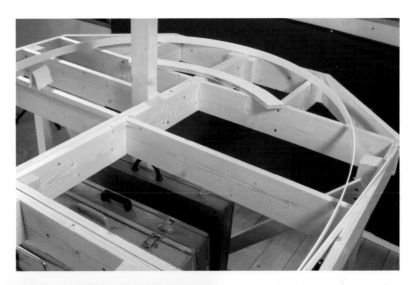

On the lower deck of the peninsula, the route of the MRL 4th Sub main line is traced in place, the curvature being checked for smooth transition from straight to curved track, using flexible plastic strip. The strip wood purchased for the project could also be used.

Temporary locating screws are fitted to the frame to hold the spine sub-road bed in place where it will eventually be required to run across the frames. After construction was complete and the spline sub-road bed fitted to risers, the screws were removed.

This picture shows the delicate task of gently but firmly shaping the first length of strip wood into place to form the turn back curve at the end of the peninsula. Will it snap? Not if the right wood is chosen, without joins and knots that would weaken it.

Two clamps at the ends hold the first spline against the temporary screws while it conforms to its new shape. It is curved but not excessively stressed.

The first spacing blocks are applied using a high quality, high-strength wood glue. Clamps hold everything in place while the glue sets. You will need a great number of clamps.

The laminations are built up a strip at a time, spacing blocks being used to save material. Experience shows that more spacing blocks are required in those areas with a sharp curve, such as at the end of the peninsula.

The spline sub-road bed is ready for its track bed which will consist of 1.5mm cork and 1mm double-sided foam tape to secure the track in place.

A single screw, driven into a countersink pilot hole is all that is required to secure the spline sub-road bed to the riser. The black mark on the baseboard frame is the original survey line made when planning the route of the track across the baseboard, so I was not too far out!

The turn back curve at the end of the peninsula is shown in this picture. The line runs from one side of the double-sided peninsula to the other at this point, leaving one scene and entering another. A double-sided backdrop will be fitted to the uprights to separate the scenes visually.

After months of using a temporary link line so the helix could be tested and a continuous run established for some operation, the main line from DesMet Junction can now continue to Frenchtown on the peninsula. The linking sub-road bed is composed of 12mm plywood. The new alignment is marked in and track laying along the lower part of the peninsula will soon begin, completing phase 1 of the MRL scheme. The temporary line curving towards the base of the helix on the left will be lifted.

LEFT: When this photograph was taken, the top deck had enjoyed some progress in the placing of track bed and the transfer of the track plan from paper to baseboards, while there was nothing on the lower deck of the peninsula to get in the way of my using it to stand on. When constructing multi-deck layouts, do as much of the messy work to the top deck that you can before working on the lower decks. When the Kent coast main line is installed, together with the Dover and Ashford staging yards, phase 1 of the top deck Folkestone East theme will be complete.

The people underpass or nod-under is given a test for comfort by my wife as she passes through following her train with Digitrax DT400 throttle firmly in hand. She is 6ft tall, yet did not find it inconvenient to use. In fact, when driving a train, the underpass turned out to be less of an inconvenience than I imagined.

CHAPTER TEN

TRACK, WIRING AND TROUBLE SHOOTING

As each stage of baseboard construction is completed and the baseboard tops (sub-road bed) fitted, track laying and wiring can commence. After all, the trains need somewhere to run.

BELOW: *It is worth looking into flooring adhesive for applying cork or foam track or road bed: it is quick with a firm hold and is permanent. Experiments with a scrap piece of plywood demonstrated how effective it can be with cork and foam, but using it with track was not so successful.*

INTRODUCTION

In building my layout in phases, track laying and wiring were undertaken at the end of each baseboard construction spree in order to get something running, otherwise it would seem that my modelling life, for some considerable time, would consist of joinery and little else owing to the size of the project. In the purest sense of layout construction, where the baseboards are built in one go, track laying, wiring, testing and other procedures, such as fitting controls, are the last stage of building the layout skeleton when all mass joinery is complete. It is important to have a reliably operating layout, bedded in and with the wrinkles worked through before starting work on the ballasting, finishing and scenery processes. Who knows what changes may need to be made to the track formation as knowledge of the layout's operations grows and its limitations are found?

On both the MRL N scale theme and Folkestone East, I am following prototype practice, with track planning based on the full size railway, so I hope that I can

lay my track in confidence that the operators of those railways got it right. Selective compression notwith-standing, so should I. No excuses!

My multi-deck layout concept was built in the phases described in Chapter 3, starting with the lower deck along the walls and fitting it with track and con-trols to get it running. Although the peninsula was not constructed until later, a temporary link line laid around the base of the helix enabled a continuous loop to be used for test running.

The second deck was built along the walls next, linking the helix and enabling some running up to it and on to a loop to test track and wiring in the helix. As the second level made up phase 2 of the N scale project, that was left for a later building session, while the peninsula was built and the joinery for the com-plete third or upper deck was built. Completing the peninsula also meant that the MRL N scale main line could be completed right round the lower level, thus completing phase 1 of that theme. The third deck could be developed too, as a two-phase project, one being Folkestone East with the other to be decided upon, although by this stage, an American HO scale (1:87.1 scale) theme based on an interchange between a com-pany called the I&M Rail Link and an interurban electric system located in Mason City, Iowa, looks favourite at the time of writing (2009).

By building in phases, the outlay on track, electrical cable and control equipment is not made all in one go and the big initial construction cost of building a lay-out is spread over a longer period of time, easing the financial stresses a little. Also, flaws in the layout design become apparent much earlier, making it easier to cor-rect them before pressing ahead with the next phase of building.

This chapter looks at track laying, together with thoughts on wiring and getting the layout running. Although my two themes are a long way from comple-tion, by the time this was being written, phase 1 of the MRL 4th Sub Division has a complete main line run of over 110ft in which to stage operating sessions and Folkestone East has its Kent Coast main line in place, allowing the operation of slam door multiple units, Channel train ferry freight and charters.

TRACK LAYING

I love laying track, working out transition curves and then watching the trains run for the first time. It is enormously satisfying! However, sound track laying depends on good preparation of the baseboard tops, track bed and, of course, a solid foundation for it all to sit on. I hope that by the time you reach this stage of your project you will have achieved all of these objectives.

Track can be fixed in place with pins, foam tape, glue or caulking products – the choices are manyfold and will depend on your preferences. But whatever you do, make it as smooth and level as you can, especially in the smaller scales. Have a thick, black marker pen to hand for marking in track centres taken from your track plan and to draw in the positions of uncoupling magnets, signals and other features that will impact on the placing of track.

A pin vice is great for holding the tiny twist drills (about 0.7mm diameter) favoured for drilling pilot holes to accept track pins. This simple precaution helps to avoid distorted sleepers and bent pins. Pliers will save you from the pain of 'fish plate finger', a malady recog-nized by my fellow modeller and good friend Graeme Elgar. Metal rail joiners or fish plates are sharp and soon make the ends of your fingers sore after an extended period of track laying.

Invest in a set of Xuron track cutters for the quick and easy cutting of rail to length. They are much more cost-effective than the use of cutting discs, which can break easily and are more hazardous to use. A small file will clean up any burrs on rail ends and can be used to lightly chamfer the ends of rails to make the fitting of rail joiners easier. So, are you ready to lay track?

SUB-ROAD BED

To recap, sub-road bed or sub-track bed is the base-board top which, in this project, is composed of either 12mm plywood, well supported, or spline road bed. Some modellers even go to plywood thicknesses of 18mm or greater, although fibre board products are avoided as much as possible because they are prone to warping, even the thicker sheets of material can bow over time. It is crucial to good track laying that you check certain things about your sub-road bed before moving on to the next layer: road or track bed:

- Check that all screws are well recessed below the surface so that they will not cause lumps in the track.
- Joins between pieces of plywood should be level; use a 'Sureform' tool to skim off any excess.
- Look for any wrinkled veneer on the surface of the plywood.
- Bowing should be corrected by adding further risers to support the sub-road bed, or the piece should be replaced altogether.
- Note any areas where spline road bed has split and make repairs with glue and screws.
- Look for any sharp changes in gradient and ease the transitions carefully by adjusting the risers.

ROAD OR TRACK BED

With the checks made to the sub-road bed, you can move on to placing the track or road bed itself. This has several important functions on my layouts and is worth including in your design, even though some modellers may not bother, to save time and material costs. The bed may be composed of cork, usually 1.5 or 3mm in thickness and depending on the scale.

Alternatively, dense and stable foam sheet is growing in popularity and that too is usually available in thicknesses of ⅛th inch or 3mm. In North America, a fibre board product called Homasote is widely used as the track bed and may be purchased ready cut into long strips, sometimes with the shoulders machined into the product.

All these materials have the following benefits, no matter which type is used:

- Track bed deadens the sound of running trains and reduces the transmission of vibration through to the timber structure of the layout.
- Track bed makes it easier to create ballast shoulders and to raise the track above the level of the baseboard tops or sub-road bed.
- Track laid on a slightly yielding surface can improve train performance.

I chose two types of road bed for my layout themes. The MRL N scale project has a layer of 1.5mm cork to create the track bed itself, including the margins either side of the line called the cess. The track was laid in strips of 1mm foam tape placed on the cork to create the ballast shoulder and to secure it in place. Off-stage areas have the track placed direct on the cork only.

The top deck Folkestone East layout has track placed on dense 3mm thick 'Plastazote' foam for its

A jigsaw is a very useful power tool for cutting shapes into sub-road bed for structures such as bridges.

sound-deadening properties. The track will be glued in place. As an aside, the portable layouts described in Chapter 5 have track placed on 3mm thick cork track bed. Experience has shown that the foam performs better, hence my choice.

The sub-road bed may be placed using a variety of glues. PVA wood glue works well on both foam and cork, although this takes time to dry and it is necessary to find something heavy with which to hold it down. Raised edges and corners are a risk with this method, but adjustments are easier to make to correct mistakes before the glue dries. High grab adhesives such as the 'No Nails' type grip the cork and foam from the start, and, although adjustments are possible, the speed at which such glues set means that you have to work fast. Flooring adhesive intended for carpet and lino products is perhaps the fastest and most secure way of placing track bed, but it grips instantaneously. Adjustments after it has grabbed are almost impossible to make.

Track or road bed may consist of one of several different materials. Sheet cork is popular with modellers because it is easy to cut and is effective at reducing vibration from running trains.

PVA wood glue is an effective way of fixing both cork and foam track bed into place. It does not bond instantly thus allowing for adjustments to be made, but the material must be held down while the glue dries.

Long sections of track bed can be cut in situ *from cork rolls to fit the sub-road bed precisely, especially if the sub-road bed is free from lots of curves. Alternatively, draw in the cut lines and make the cuts with a steel rule on the work bench.*

Flooring adhesive is very effective in placing cork and most especially foam track bed, as it bonds instantly and permanently. However, removal of the track bed to make adjustments, especially if it has been in place for more than 5min, is difficult. The adhesive is sprayed on from a height of about 10in until the baseboard top has an even coat. It is left for 5min for the adhesive to go tacky before you lay the track bed.

The track bed is carefully laid on the baseboard top or sub-road bed to avoid ripples, trapped air and to ensure that it is in the right place.

Before track laying, examine the cork track bed for unevenness, lifted corners and edges that have refused to stick down properly. Smooth off imperfections with sanding paper wrapped around a cork block.

BELOW: One way of avoiding glue or the use of track pins, which looks unsightly, is to fix small gauge track in place using double-sided, self-adhesive foam tape, which provides a strong bond and quieter running.

BEFORE YOU LAY TRACK ...

Give consideration to any uncoupling system that you may wish to use. Kadee and similar delayed magnetic systems are growing in popularity in the UK. In North America they are standard for most modellers. When drawing in the centre line of the track, work out exactly where uncoupling magnets are to go, allowing for the length of locomotives and the rolling stock vehicles. Install them before laying the track because a retrospective installation is likely to be messy, expensive and disruptive. They should be incorporated into the track plan at the layout design stage and added to the project list, so that they are not forgotten.

Ensure that you have enough hardware supplies to hand. Stock up on the appropriate rail joiners, glue, tape and track pins before you start, because I find that, once I start on a track laying session, I like to make good progress. Running out of essential items such as rail joiners is a bore when in the middle of a good session.

INSTALLING KADEE MAGNETS

All of my collection of British and North American models are fitted with knuckle couplings, so before laying track on my layouts I gave careful thought to the uncoupling devices I wished to use. Kadee couplings

are fitted to my British outline 4mm-scale locomotives and rolling stock, so the appropriate delayed action uncoupling devices are installed on my EM gauge layouts, including the portable layout, Dudley Heath Yard. Retrospectively fitting such uncoupling magnets after the track has been placed and ballasted can be nearly impossible without destroying a lot of careful work. I decided against using permanent magnetic uncouplers, such as the Kadee Nos. 308 and 321, preferring a type which can be electronically controlled. The

electromagnet type for use with Kadees and designed to sit between the rails, the No. 307, has been super-seded by the No. 309 'Under-the-Ties' electromagnet uncoupler, which was my preferred choice for Dudley Heath Yard.

Similar delayed-action magnetic uncoupling systems are available for US-outline N scale modelling, offered by Micro Trains, to match its range of knuckle couplings. They are mostly based on permanent magnets rather than electromagnets.

The preference of most modellers is to conceal the magnets under the track and ballast so that there is no visual impact. To do this involves the construction technique shown in the accompanying illustrations.

There is a variety of different magnetic uncoupling systems available, and sometimes the choice from one manufacturer alone may be more than enough. The Kadee products shown in this picture are intended for HO scale and may be used for British outline OO gauge models too. Only one of the four shown is designed for fitting between the rails, the No. 321 magnetic uncoupler, which can be retrospectively installed in an established layout without the need to lift any track.

RIGHT: *This picture shows a No. 309 electromagnet fully assembled and ready for installation. Its location needs to be carefully chosen to avoid baseboard joists and so it is located where it will be most effective during operations.*

When transferring the track plan to the layout, the centre line for each track is drawn in with a black marker pen. Use the longest locomotive to determine clearances and the best location for uncoupling devices. The

location marked (A) was determined to be ideal, based on the length of the Hornby Class 60 and the distance from a turnout fouling point at (B).

RIGHT: A hole is drilled out through the baseboard top by using a 10mm-diameter wood drill. Drilling a network of holes makes the cutting and finishing of the hole easier than using a jigsaw.

Another technique to cut a precise hole is to use a junior hacksaw blade to cut the drill holes together. At all times use the assembled uncoupler to check the size and shape of the hole.

Cleaning up with a chisel: keep fingers and hands behind the blade just in case it slips.

The uncoupling device is fitted to the baseboard by screwing its top plate in place. Note how the cork road bed has been cut to shape to accommodate it so that there is a flat surface for laying track.

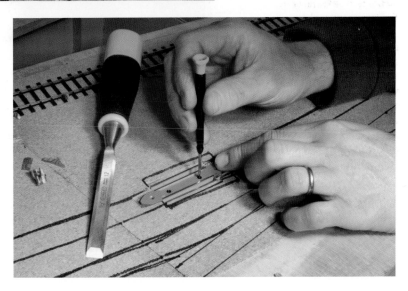

Further material can be removed from the baseboard top as shown at (X) to add to the recess that the uncoupling device occupies below the level of the cork road bed.

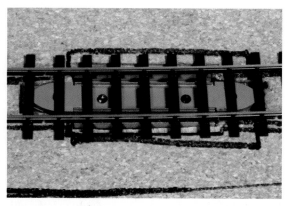

The device correctly fitted, as seen in this photograph. The track is placed over it to check that there are no raised parts that may cause problems.

When the position and the fitting of the device are satisfactory, it is covered with a piece of silver foil before track is fixed permanently over the top of it. This will prevent rail ballast and glue from making a mess of the device and it also means that the device will be easier to recover for reuse when the layout is retired and dismantled. The device is operated with push-to-make buttons.

CHOOSING TRACK

Another area of debate and needing decision making is in the choice and preference of track. There is a huge variety of track products available and to make a choice is not always easy. I use track that looks good to me and has a good reputation with other modellers. A simple guide regarding choosing track is as follows:

Find out which track is most appropriate for your layout theme. If modelling the steam era in the UK, it is likely that bull head rail will be the most appropriate. Modern-era modellers could have a mix of rail types, including bull head rail and modern flat bottom, on their layouts. Main lines and heavily used tracks will be fitted with heavier flat bottom rail, while many yards and sidings in the UK continued to see the use of often second-hand bull head rail. North American modellers will exclusively use flat bottom rail track, the size being dependent on the type of railroad and whether it is a main line, siding or a spur.

Rail size is important and model railway codes its track depending on size: code 55 rail is smaller and finer than code 100. The latter may be popular with main line trackage in HO scale, while code 83 is often the choice for more lightly used lines. In N scale, code 80 is popular, although code 55 track is growing in popularity for its finer appearance. The code number indicates the height of the rail as a fraction of an inch. For example, the popular code 100 rail is 100 thousands of an inch (so 100×0.001 in). For more information on rail codes, look at the NMRA recommended practice No. RP-15.1. This may be read at *www.nmra.org/standards/sandrp/rp-15_1.html*

Check that the track system you wish to use has the turnout and crossing sizes you need to fit your layout plan.

Set track or flexi-track? You can mix both on a lay-out provided that the rail code and shape are the same and, ideally, that they are from the same track system. I used Atlas code 55 flexi track on the MRL N scale layout almost exclusively, except for some curves and on the helix where I relied on set track curves from the same range to make track laying easier.

Build your own: templates for hand-built track in most scales are available, as are track and turnout kits. Fast Tracks of Canada offer a wide range of turnout and crossing kits for North American practice, including some useful track-shaping and filing tools. In the UK, C&L Finescale offer turnout kits for OO gauge and the closer to scale gauges such as EM and P4. The range includes laser-cut track templates and pre-formed track components, together with chairs and sleepers for a variety of different types of plain track. The Folkestone East theme on my layout uses its code 75 bull head flexi-track in the staging yards and yard sidings.

Peco offers a range of track components called 'Individulay', which can be used to make up bespoke track formations to HO, OO, EM and P4 gauges. The components can be used in conjunction with flexi track and turnout products such as the Peco Code 83 line for North American practice. They include sleepers, 'Pandrol' clip fixings, conductor rail insulators and turnout components as well as track detailing items.

FIXING THE TRACK IN PLACE

I do not like to use track pins in the scenic sections of a layout. I prefer to use double-sided foam tape to apply the fine code 55 Atlas track on the MRL N scale project and glue to secure the flexi track panels on the British EM gauge theme. It is a different matter in off-stage areas where track pins are used widely on both themes as their unsightly heads do not spoil photography, partly for speed and partly so that the track can be lifted and reused.

In the past, I have used track pins in scenic areas of layouts, removing them once the ballast was placed and glued down. The tiny holes could still be seen, but are easily filled with paint to remove their visual impact, especially in photographs. Here are some of the more popular track-fixing techniques:

- Track pins: easily fitted to predrilled pilot holes – the finer the pin, the better. Support them with fine nose pliers when driving them home to prevent them from bending. There are a variety of special pin-driving tools which can be used and they are worth investing in if there is a lot of track to lay using this method. Avoid them in scenic areas or remove them once ballast has been placed and the glue dry. Track pins are easily removed to allow the realignment of track or its complete removal while avoiding excessive damage to the track itself.
- PVA wood glue: use a waterproof type of wood glue and spread it over the track or road bed with a spatula before laying the track. Depending on the type and the conditions, it can take time to dry, so the track should be held down temporarily with pins or some heavy objects.
- Firm grip glues and caulks: they offer a quick grab to secure your carefully calculated alignments and the track will be well secured thereafter too. Removal without destroying the track will be difficult and realignment, should an error in track laying occur, will be equally awkward to correct, so be sure to get your alignment right first time. A bead of glue is applied from the glue or caulk gun and spread evenly with a spatula or scrap piece of wood. Press the track into place, hopefully

avoiding too much glue from squeezing up between the sleepers. It is a great method for placing track for HO and OO gauge, especially code 100 track, but may be a little more awkward for finer track with thin sleepers or N scale track.

● Foam tape is an instant way of laying track without the mess of glue or the use of unsightly pins. However, its instant grab makes adjustment difficult and lifting track after a period of time is nearly impossible without damage. The foam further deadens the sound of running trains and creates a useful raised track bed for realistic ballast shoulders.

● When laying track check the instructions supplied with your turnouts to see whether an insulating rail joiner is required at the diverging side of the crossing vee (frog). This is usually the case with Peco Electro frog turnouts, for example.

● Long runs of running line, which use a full length of flexi track, should have small gaps in the rail at each rail joiner to allow for expansion, should the layout room become warm during the summer. Gauge the need for expansion gaps on the day with regard to the ambient temperature at the time and the time of year.

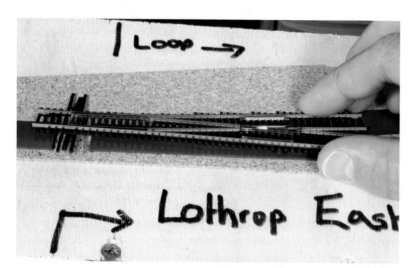

Track laying is an enjoyable but critical part of building the structure of a layout. The modeller must be aware of the need to use rail joiners in the right places and to ensure that turnout mechanisms do not become damaged with glue. Note that a gap has been left in the foam tape to clear the switch mechanism of this Atlas Code 55 turnout.

A hole must be drilled through the baseboard top so that the activation wire of a Tortoise point motor will reach the turnout switch. The precise position is marked in with a black pen.

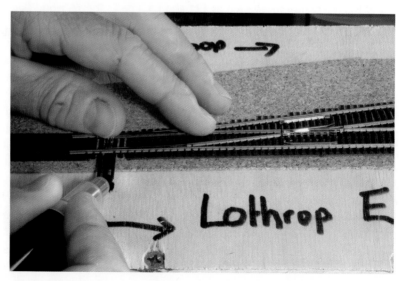

A 10mm-diameter hole is drilled through the baseboard top ready for installing the turnout machine. This would be difficult to do if the turnout had been stuck down and track leading to it fixed in place. It is important, as a result, to plan ahead and work out those tasks you need to do before track laying.

The protective film is removed from the foam tape used on the N scale MRL layout only when all the other preparation is finished. The track is fitted to the now revealed and very sticky surface of the tape.

The turnout, which forms the end of a passing loop or siding at a location on the layout called Lothrop, is shown fixed in place, with the hole for the turnout machine activation wire located precisely under the stretcher bar.

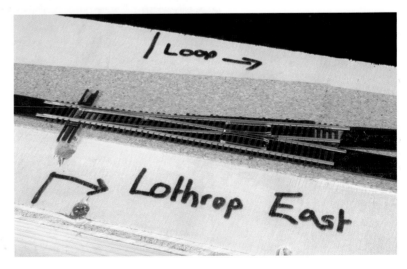

Plain flexi track for the passing loop roads is prepared by removing the rail clips from the first two sleepers (ties) so that metal rail joiners can be easily slipped into place.

The flexi track is carefully connected to the turnout by using the metal rail joiners so that a smooth join between the rails is achieved. Take care not to slide a rail joiner under the adjacent rail, which would cause a step in the join and, inevitably, derailments. Some makes of turnout require the use of an insulating rail joiner on the rails diverging from the crossing vee to prevent short circuits.

Flexi track can be cut to length to suit the required track formation. Some of the most useful tools a modeller can invest in are Xuron track cutters. They save a considerable amount of time and are safer to use than cutting discs.

Some modellers prefer to use track pins throughout their layouts. It is good practice to drill pilot holes through the sleeper and part way into the track bed to help to drive the pins into place without them bending.

When choosing track, the modeller is not restricted to using flexi track or set track pieces. Some manufacturers such as C&L Finescale, Peco, Exactoscale and Fast Tracks (Canada) offer track-building components for bespoke formations. This picture shows Peco Individulay sleepers being laid on cork by using wood glue on Dudley Heath Yard.

A bead of glue is applied to the cork road bed and spread out with a spatula (a piece of wood or cardboard) before the sleepers are carefully laid in place, one by one.

Both concrete and wooden-style sleepers are available in 4mm-scale for British outline modellers. You may also be able to find laser-cut plywood sleepers too. Once the glue has dried, the rail is fitted by using plastic rail fixings or, in the case of plywood sleepers, rail pins.

LAYOUT WIRING

At the very beginning of my project, I planned to use Digital Command Control throughout, and chose Digitrax for my US outline N scale project, while keeping with Lenz for the British layout. Wiring for both themes is essentially the same, consisting of two power bus wires running from the rear of the base station through the length of the layout to supply dropper wires connected to the track. I do not wire the power bus in a circle or closed loop, but follow the practice of radial wiring runs down each arm of the layout, terminating them at the end of each base-board. The power bus wires are kept as short as possible to reduce voltage drop. The following conditions were met during the wiring of the layout:

Power bus cable consists of high-grade, stranded copper wire capable of carrying at least 5A. My choice for the layout where the longest power bus cable run of

Useful supplies for wiring the layout with a DCC power bus: 24/0.2 grade cable, as seen on the reels, which is capable of carrying at least 5A, single-strand bell wire for droppers to link the power bus to the track and a good pair of wire strippers (to save your teeth!).

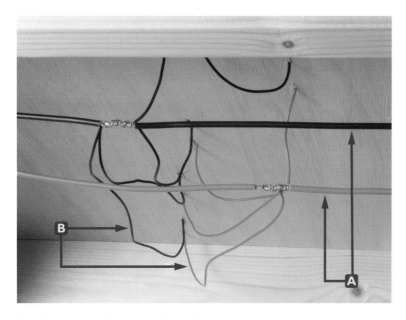

The simplest of power bus wiring is shown in this photograph. The large power bus cables (A) run the length of the layout from the DCC base station. The smaller diameter wires are dropper wires that connect to the track (B). Each length of rail is supplied with current so there is no reliance on rail joiners as far as possible.

BELOW: *The helix on the N scale layout has the power bus running up the sides, the red outer rail wire up the outside and, correspondingly, the black wire up the inside. Each level of the helix has a power supply and any rail joiners likely to cause a problem are soldered.*

20ft is 24/0.2, although 32/0.2 would be better for runs longer than my 20ft maximum.

Single-strand bell wire is connected to each length of rail. It can carry at least 1A and its stiffness makes it easy to solder to the running rail and make a good connection with the power bus. Dropper wires should be no longer than 4in from power bus to rail; do not rely on rail joiners to carry current.

Nickel-silver rail has a relatively higher resistance to current over copper wire. Do not rely on the rail to carry the digital signal and full current strength to remote parts of the layout. Extend the power bus run instead and ensure that you provide plenty of connections between the power bus and track.

A circuit breaker was used to separate the power bus runs for the two decks of the N scale layout into sub-power districts. This protects one circuit from short circuits on the other, should a derailment occur. Such power management is important on a larger layout. It can be extended to include additional boosters to create power districts for better distribution of enough power around the layout to overcome long runs of power bus voltage drop and high current consumption when many locomotives are in use.

Connections between the power bus and dropper wires can be easily made by using 'suitcase' connectors.

Setting up the control system takes time and care, not to mention frequent reference to the manuals supplied with the system. This is a close-up view of a power management module which is supplied by Digitrax. It is a PM42 Power Manager, capable of handling four power sub-districts. Those sub-districts may be large areas of the layout or reverse loops. The complete assembly was being tested and programmed when this photograph was taken.

With all testing of the control equipment complete, it can be carefully placed on the layout in an off-stage area where access to it is straightforward. The power manager is located on the wall where its indicator LEDs can be clearly seen and the wiring neatly arranged. Note that all power bus cable runs have labels to identify them. Also noteworthy is the use of a document holder to keep all the necessary instruction manuals together and conveniently to hand.

I prefer to strip about 12mm of insulation from the bus wire and wrap 15mm of stripped dropper wire around it to make a solid connection. It should be flooded with solder once all the required connections are made, then covered with insulation tape should the risk of its touching any other power source be likely.

Some Tortoise turnout motors are controlled through the power bus and stationary decoder together with conventional button control. Others on the layout are simply controlled by using DPDT switches grouped on a local control panel.

For more detail on wiring a layout for Digital Command Control, and how to use the system for effective train driving and operational detailing, refer to my *Practical Introduction to Digital Command Control for Railway Modellers* (Crowood).

THOUGHTS ON CONTROL

The whole approach to layout control, for me, is to keep signalling and turnout control as simple as possible. I planned for a light, relatively low-tech, soft touch on route setting for both my MRL N scale and Folkestone East too, rather than construct something that is hugely complicated to build, operate and maintain. Mainline turnouts for loops and crossovers are operated with Tortoise point motors, controlled from local panels situated at strategic points around the layout; yard tracks will be manually controlled by using ground throws. After all, for me the enjoyment of a layout is to run trains, not to play signalman.

I have noticed, as Digital Command Control and wireless hand-held DCC controllers (throttles) become increasingly mainstream, the method of layout operation in which you follow the train around the layout, rather than operate it from a fixed position, has become ever more popular. This means a change in the way that people organize control panels for turnouts and signals. Rather than operate the layout from a complex, central panel, which, in the case of some layouts, appears to have a complexity equal to that of the computers used to launch the space shuttle, it is sometimes useful to have local panels for the control of turnouts leading to a yard, a loop or an industrial siding of some description.

By using DCC throttles on my project, together with the walk-round driving of trains, control is more localized around the layout, which prevents congestion around a main control panel when more than two operators are involved with an operating session. Furthermore, it also means that an individual shunting a yard or an industrial siding does not have to return to a central control panel every time a turnout needs to be changed. Another method of localized control is to assign DCC decoders to each turnout motor or solenoid so that points can be changed by using the digital handset or throttle instead of throwing a switch on a control panel. This can be done anywhere, but at the expense of accessory decoders and less co-ordinated control in some instances.

This idea can be as flexible as one wishes: a network of localized panels around the layout but still have a main signal and turnout panel, which is operated by a signalman, for example. The main panel would be equipped with lockout switches that could prevent the local panels from being used, for the control of turnouts on the main line. The idea can be made more technical by displaying and controlling the main panel on a personal computer or laptop connected to a DCC command station by using a PC interface device and accessory decoders for turnout control. A central route-setting function is created, with a degree of automation if desired, controlled by the person nominated as signalman, which can be changed when local control is required.

The Folkestone East theme has the controls grouped at the front of the layout because that is where all the action is to be found and the MRL N scale layout has several local panels located around the layout, together with Digitrax UR90 Infra-red connection panels for plugging throttles into or for wireless infra-red operation. This arrangement prevents congestion between operators driving the N scale trains on the lower decks and anyone driving trains on Folkestone East. The following example of a localized control point, consisting of a Digitrax UR90 and a small turnout control panel, controls the junction at the west end of Missoula Yard (West Missoula) on the MRL N scale layout. The panel was built to the following dimensions:

- length of styrene panel front: 270mm;
- width of styrene panel front: 110mm;
- width from front of layout fascia to front of the top edge of panel: 10mm;
- width from front of layout fascia to front of the bottom edge of panel: 40mm;
- 8mm holes drilled to accept DPDT switches;
- 5.5mm holes drilled to accept LEDs and grommets;
- 2mm holes drilled to accept self-tapping screws.

The size can be adapted to suit almost any situation, given that everyone's layout will be unique in many ways. A very small panel could be constructed to house a single switch to control a reversing loop or turnout, for example, or a long one for a complex junction or yard throat.

LEFT: Another important wiring task is to install the DCC controller bus. This is a network of cables and connectors independent of the power bus and not connected to it. It enables connector panels to be fitted around the layout so that the hand controllers can be plugged in at convenient points of operation.

ABOVE: The outline of the connector panels is drawn on the layout fascia and a hole large enough to accommodate the circuit board drilled out, as shown in this picture.

The rough hole is cut to shape and smoothed to remove rough edges and splinters. Use the connector panel to gently check the size of the hole as you work.

Screw holes are marked in with a pencil so that a shallow pilot hole can be drilled in the right place before the panel is fitted by using self-tapping screws.

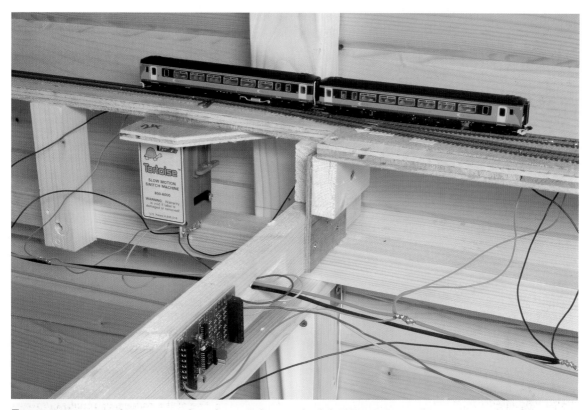

Tortoise turnout machines are used on the main line track of the N scale layout. This one is connected to a DCC decoder, which allows the turnout to be operated by using the throttle in addition to push-button control. A Dapol Class 156 enjoys a run over the N scale layout and is seen passing over the powered turnout.

RIGHT: A position on the front fascia of the layout is carefully chosen for the location of local control panels so that they are as close to the junction or industry spur they serve as possible, yet are unlikely to cause an obstruction in the aisle. The frame consists of off-cuts of planed wood which are glued and clamped to the front fascia. The size of each piece is important so that a sloped panel front results and there is room for the electrical wiring behind it. This panel was to be fitted with DPDT switches for controlling Tortoise switch machines.

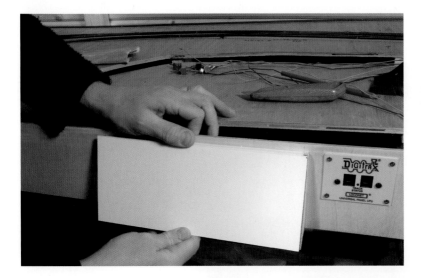

Panel fronts may be made from almost any material, including white-faced hardboard, 6mm plywood, acetate sheet, styrene sheet or any sort of plastic sheet that takes your fancy, or anything you happen to have lying around. They may be any colour you like, as long as they are thick enough to support the switches and LEDs without bowing or distortion.

Holes are drilled through the back of the control panel and through the fascia so that the wiring could be fed through to the turnout motors from the switches. The holes were located to avoid drilling through the L-girder baseboard frame behind the fascia.

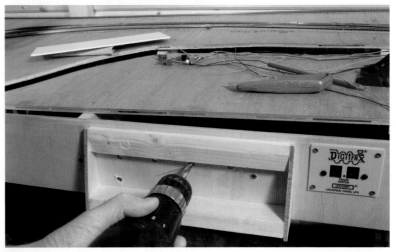

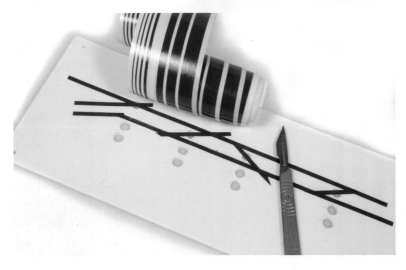

Model aircraft trim tape is an ideal medium for depicting the track layout on the panel front because it is usually strongly self-adhesive and available in a variety of bright colours. The trim tape is placed on the panel front, as shown. Choose different thicknesses of line to imply the importance of individual lines, such as the main line, sidings and loops.

Fitting out the control panel face was done at the workbench, where the DPDT switch (A) mounting holes of 8mm diameter (B) are drilled precisely in place on the line diagram (C); 5mm LEDs (D) are fitted to mounting grommets (E) before installation in 5.5mm holes.

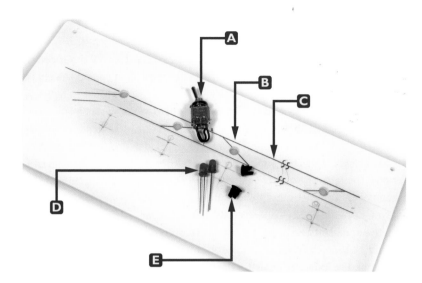

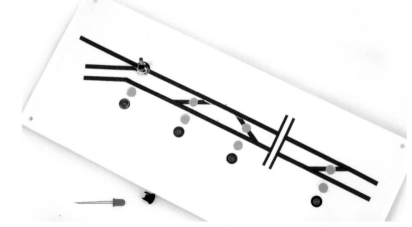

The panel is coming along nicely with electrical components installed. Wiring will be next and most of that is done at the work bench before the assembly is transferred to the layout and the wiring is connected to a power supply and the Tortoise turnout motors.

A perfect fit with all electrical connections hooked up and working. The switch on the far right controls a pair of turnouts remote from this panel, duplicating the controls on another. At the time of writing (2009), the track was still to be placed at that remote location, hence the indicator LEDs are dark. The panel frame may be painted the same colour as the fascia, which is in a contrasting colour to the panel front when layout construction reaches that stage of finishing.

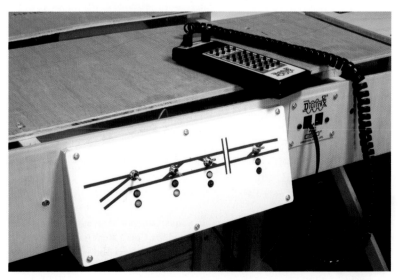

MAINTENANCE AND CLEANING

KEEPING THE LAYOUT AND TRACK CLEAN

Dirty track, better described as dirty rail, is blamed for a host of ills, especially on poor performing exhibition layouts. One of those famous (or infamous) model railway black arts has grown and prospered from the various opinions of how to deal with dirty rail. The extent of the problem and how it impacts on your enjoyment of the hobby depends on a number of factors, the dominant one being the actual size of the layout and how much track is actually on it. The bigger the layout, the longer it takes to clean the dirt away and I don't need to repeat to experienced modellers that rail cleaning is a tedious, time-consuming and boring task.

Without removing the gunk that builds up on the top and the side of the running rail, the operation of model railways becomes disjointed, dissatisfying and certainly unconvincing. Dirt has a nasty habit of striking at any time. It does so when we are in the process of displaying our treasured models either to the public or to a group of (usually influential) friends. There is a direct relationship between the importance of those viewing the layout, together with the level of impression we wish to make, and how quickly and intensively track dirt decides to strike. Once it does so, it is pretty decisive, bringing trains to a standstill, causing flickering lights and digital sound decoders to stutter and stall. Prodding our models back into life with a finger is no

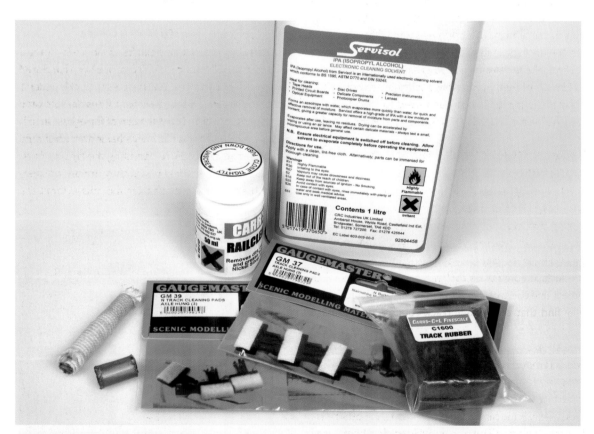

A selection of materials used to clean the rails: Gaugemaster/Noch track-cleaning pads have grown in popularity as have chemical dirt-repellent materials such as Carr's Railclean. Isopropyl alcohol (IPA) is an excellent material to have available for cleaning rails, wheels, mechanisms and electrical equipment. Have some plastic pipettes to hand for dispensing small quantities of cleaning fluids.

way to make an impression on exhibition visitors or friends during a running evening at home.

How does one separate the elements of black magic from what are successful methods of removing dirt from the rails? The methods employed by an individual modeller will much depend on what the dirt actually is. From my own experience, that material broadly classified as 'dirt' that ends up on the surface of the rail comes from several sources. First, dust from the atmosphere in the layout room, which can include skin cells among other things, will accumulate on the rail surface over time, becoming compacted into a strange compound, the nature of which is best left to the imagination. Dust covers can do much to prevent unwanted dust settling on the layout.

Sometimes, work on the layout means that paint, sawdust and glue may be introduced to the surface of the rail and these will not conduct electricity. It is likely that material from traction tyres and lubricants from model mechanisms will also make their way on to the surface of the rails. Tarnished rails resulting from the oxidation of metal inevitably occurs over time, especially if the layout is not been used for a while, and they definitely disrupt the passage of electricity.

TRACK CLEANING METHODS
Track rubbers

By their very nature, track rubbers are abrasive in action, working on the surface of the rail. It is worth noting that cleaning the inside edge of the rail is as important as cleaning the top surface. Track rubbers generally do not get the inside edge, working only on the surface. Some track rubbers are more abrasive than others and users of fine scale rail or N gauge modellers may find that the harder track rubbers may damage the surface of the rail. Modellers with overhead electrification or numerous over bridges on their layouts will find that track rubbers cannot reach all of the rail head. If this type of cleaning method suits your layout, cut a small piece from a block and attach to a stick. The modified rubber can be used to reach those otherwise inaccessible areas. The two popular track rubbers used in the UK include the hard Peco track rubber which is quite abrasive in its action and the softer C&L Finescale rubber, which is sold under the Carr's label. They are

invaluable for removing hardened dirt from the surface of the rail such as glue and paint appearing after a scenery modelling session.

Abrasive paper

Abrasive papers, such as wet and dry paper, are excellent for removing burrs and hardened dirt from the rails, especially after a work session on the layout. I use grade 800 wet and dry paper in the dry state to ensure that there are no rough edges left on the cut ends of rail after track laying. I wrap a small amount of the paper around a track rubber and use it gently to polish the surface of the rail. The finer grades wet and dry paper won't damage the rail surface if they are used gently. It is important to remember that the profile of the rail is important to the handling of trains and their ability to stay on the rails.

Fibre scratch pencils

A gently abrasive cleaning can be achieved by using a fibreglass pencil or stick. It will remove both hardened and chemical dirt from the track very quickly, indeed, and the rails tend to stay clean for a considerable time afterwards. It is noted that the use of fibreglass pencils or sticks may leave small filaments behind, which should be vacuumed away before operating the layout. However, unlike hard track rubbers, they are an inexpensive and effective way of cleaning the rails without the

Fibre sticks are an effective and gentle abrasive cleaning action that will not wear the rail down; they also clean the edges of the rail.

String bound fibre sticks are effective rail cleaners and can shift glue, paint and other contaminants resulting from layout building; remove the fibre dross after cleaning.

The good old fashioned track rubber. This is a gentle version produced by C&L Finescale and sold under the Carr's label.

risk of damaging the railhead. On personal experience, this abrasive method is certainly easier on the track than the use of track rubbers. Angling the fibreglass stick also means that you can get at the inside edge of the railhead, thus ensuring that your cleaning action is as efficient as possible.

Alcohol and cloth

Isopropyl alcohol (IPA) is an extremely effective chemical cleaner. Apply a small amount to a lint-free cloth, which will not leave fabric fibres on the track, and gently rub the rail using your finger until the cloth becomes dirty. Soak a new area of the cloth and repeat the process. It is amazing how much black gunk is removed from the rails by using this technique. When compared to fibreglass pencils and track rubbers, this method of cleaning is the most effective in what is called the 'white glove test', in which a piece of dry white cloth is rubbed along the rails to see how much black is removed. However, for large layouts this method is both tedious and time-consuming. The solution for larger layouts would be to use IPA in some sort of automated track cleaning system, such as a track cleaning vehicle or the axle hung pads offered by Noch and marketed in the UK by Gaugemaster. Modellers should note that IPA can damage acrylic paint finishes.

Specific chemical cleaners

There are a number of products available that have a chemical action on the rails to ensure that electrical contact is made between the wheels and the rails. The agent is applied to the rails and either carried round by the running of trains or applied wet from a cloth over the whole layout and then allowed to dry. An example of the former is a product from the US called Rail Zip. While I have experienced success with this, there have been reports from some modellers that Rail Zip can affect traction tyres and some plastic wheel sets; C&L Finescale offers its Railclean product which works by forming an electrically-conductive salt on the rail, which also improves adhesion between the wheel and the rail. This product appears to have an excellent record and is particularly popular with modellers in the UK.

Electronic track cleaners

High-frequency, electronic track cleaners have been available for the use on analogue layouts for some time, and one well-known brand that proved very popular was Relco. They work by providing an electrical method of maintaining conductivity between the wheel and rail. Unfortunately, the majority of these products are not compatible with Digital Command Control because electronic track cleaners can disrupt the digital signal between the command station and decoders on a DCC layout, together with blasting decoders with high voltage. Furthermore, decoder-equipped locomotives operated on analogue layouts which are fitted with such electronic track cleaners may suffer damage. An exception to this are Elektrack products. Nonetheless, DCC-users should approach this subject with caution and seek advice from their suppliers.

Bespoke mobile cleaning devices

Track-cleaning cars are growing in popularity, even though they cost considerably more than the tradition-al track rubber; they are either propelled or hauled by a locomotive and may be left to circulate the lay-out, run into sidings and through passing loops until the layout owner is satisfied that the rails are sufficient-ly clean for a trouble-free operating session. Some track-cleaning cars also incorporate a permanent mag-net that will pick up any stray track pins or other fer-rous objects that could be attracted into a locomotive mechanism by the magnet on the motor. They may be placed in one of two categories: there are the mechanical types, which include the Tomix and Dapol OO/HO gauge track-cleaning car, and passive types that do not use any motor or mechanism to provide

a scrubbing action to the rails. The mechanical track-cleaning cars are equipped with an electronic mecha-nism or some form of unpowered mechanism that provides a mechanical scrubbing action to the rails to remove dirt. Clearly, something that has any sort of mechanism will cost a great deal more than a bottle of chemical cleaner or a track rubber. However, they are particularly attractive to operators of large lay-outs where there is a great deal of rail to clean and little time to spend cleaning it. Track-cleaning vehicles have done much to save time and this is the reason why they have become increasingly popular over the years. Passive track-cleaning cars simply rely on a reservoir to contain a cleaning solvent, which is gravity-fed to a track-cleaning pad underneath the vehicle.

In a sense, some products act both as a chemical and an abrasive cleaner, depending very much on the one that you choose. For example, the Tomix and Dapol track-cleaning cars are abrasive in their action, although that action is both gentle and effective. Other such vehicles include the Centreline Products cars, which use a non-abrasive roller action in which a spindle is fitted with a fabric roll, in effect another mechanical cleaning method.

The CMX Clean Machine is modelled like a tank wagon with a brass tank for holding a cleaning solvent,

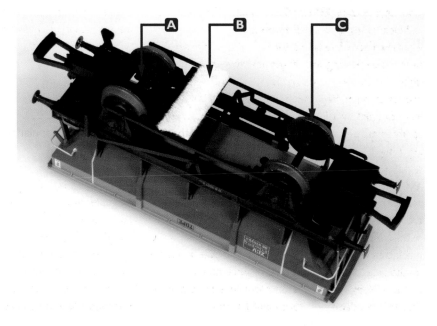

This view of a Hornby 'Tope' ballast wagon shows how the pads clip to the axle (A). There must be sufficient room under the wagon to allow the soft pad (B) to rest on the track without pressure from brake gear or hopper chutes. Place a small drop of IPA on the pad to encourage the cleaning of the rails. Note the paint on the wheel tyre (C), clean this away to help to keep the rails clean.

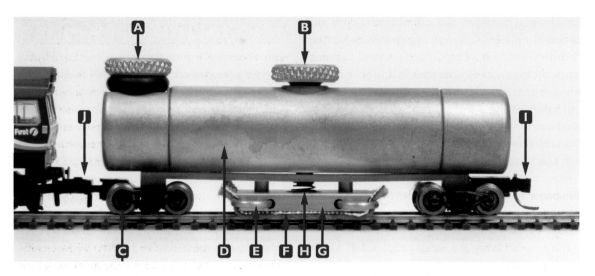

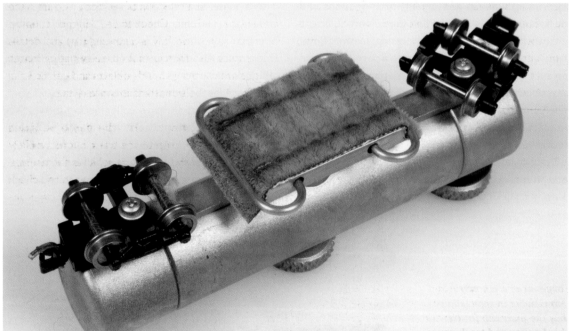

TOP: *The CMX Clean Machine track-cleaning car is my preferred choice for cleaning the rails on the MRL N scale layout. It is suitable for the British outline N gauge too, and versions for HO/OO gauge and O gauge are also available. It has some interesting features: (A) filler hatch with rubber seal; (B) solvent-dispensing release valve; (C) durable bogies with metal wheels that will not be affected by chemical cleaners; (D) brass reservoir tank for holding the cleaning solvent; (E) cleaning-pad retaining clip; (F) cleaning pad – cloth for use with solvent; (G) weighted and sprung pad holder; (H) base of the dispensing that is adjusted to control the 'drip rate'; (I) different couplers fitted to the N scale version to suit various locomotives; (J) Rapido type coupling fitted to the opposite end, which suits Graham Farish models.*

BOTTOM: *A view of the underside of the CMX Clean Machine showing the cloth pad in place. The solvent drip rate should be fast enough to keep the pad wet and prevent the solvent from running along the bottom of the tank barrel by capillary action, but not so fast as to flood the track.*

a filler and a gravity-feed valve that soaks a cloth pad fitted to the underside. The pad holder is weighted so that the pad itself rubs against the rails, cleaning as it is propelled by a locomotive. The CMX Clean Machine may also be fitted with a piece of wet and dry paper for abrasive cleaning. It is quite an effective vehicle in all scales from N gauge to G scale. However, its brass construction makes it an expensive option.

A similar car to the CMX Clean Machine is the Trackman 2000, which is a passive track-cleaning car featuring a similar weighted rubbing block that holds an abrasive track rubber. It is more economical that the CMX Clean Machine and available in Z, N, HO/OO and O gauges. However, it does not offer a chemical cleaning option.

Choosing between these mobile cleaning devices will depend upon the budget, type of cleaning you desire and other practical issues. For example, the Tomix, Dapol and Trackman 2000 types do not rely on liquid solvents which can spill and cause damage. The CMX Clean Machine and similar types are fitted with weighted rubbing pads, which could catch detail associated with the track, such as a conductor rail. However, mobile cleaners are great for dealing with tunnels, hidden trackage, overhead line equipment and delicate semaphore signal gantries where it is more awkward to use a manual cleaning method.

DEALING WITH DERAILMENTS

Nothing destroys the enthusiasm for operating a layout more than derailments. Not the occasional one – for that happens to full-size railways from time to time – but what my friend Graeme Elgar calls an 'earth fault' soon becomes disheartening if it happens on a more than occasional basis. It was to avoid these that I spent so much of the layout design time working out the minimal track curvature that my trains would have to cope with and carefully applying that to my design.

When derailments occur, watch the performance of trains carefully over trouble spots with the vehicles with which the problem occurs. Look for wheel sets lifting over rails and check whether the derailments are random with just a selection of vehicles or occur in the same place randomly. Check to see whether coupling trip pins are not too low and striking rails and details on the track. Also, look carefully to see whether longer vehicles are touching lineside objects and details. Let's take a look at the symptoms in more detail:

Random derailments with the same vehicles
Clearly, this is not down to the track, but more likely to be the fault of the individual vehicles themselves. Remove from the layout to the work bench and check to see whether the underframe, trucks or bogies are

Gauges are a very important item to have in your tool box. They are essential for checking wheel gauge and track gauge to ensure that they meet the specifications for your chosen scale and gauge. The tool used to check the measurement of wheels is called a 'back-to-back' gauge and saves a great deal of trouble with derailments. Roller gauges are used to check the distance between rails and to see whether they are in gauge. They may also be used to check turnout flange ways.

square with all wheels sitting on a sheet of glass. If a three-legged effect is seen, with one wheel in the air, that's the answer to the problem. Failing that, check the distance between the wheels, known as the back-to-back measurement. You should buy a 'back-to-back' gauge to check this distance. Usually, even a slight difference in this measurement will cause derailments, especially through turnout flange ways.

Derailments in the same places with randomly selected vehicles It's a track fault if the problem occurs in the same place. It could be out of gauge or uneven. Check with a roller gauge and make adjustments where necessary to correct any misalignment. Uneven track can be packed with shims of styrene, if it has not already been ballasted, to level the running rail. Canting or elevating the track on curves using

shims of 10 thou and 20 thou styrene is also very effective at eliminating derailments. Examine rail joiners for burrs and smooth them away with grade 800 emery paper for a smooth rail surface. Do the same with switch blades in turnouts to ensure the smooth passage of wheels into turnouts.

Couplings Such items can droop and catch the running rail or other details, causing derailments. Check poorly performing vehicles for low trip pins or couplings that have come loose and may be dragging on the track. It is also worth noting where sharp curves may be beyond the reach of couplings on longer cars, so consider fitting a longer type of coupling or a different type capable of keeping vehicle buffers, gangways and similar features from catching on each other and throwing one or both vehicles off the track.

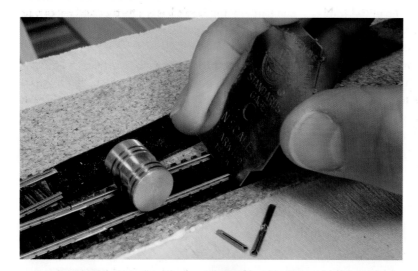

An NMRA gauge and a roller gauge are demonstrated checking the distance between the rails on a length of flexi track. Persistent derailments at one location on a layout often suggest problems with the track and gauges such as these can often help to locate the problem.

Modellers who build their own track from kits and templates will use roller gauges to fit the rails to specification and to achieve smooth running and reliable track. This is an example of a C&L Finescale Timber Track laser-cut template fitted with the company's rails fixings and bull head rail.

AND FINALLY ...

The first run! Running trains for the first time on any completed layout phase is a very exciting time. With all that careful planning, construction, testing, track checking, wheel back-to-back measuring and so on, the first run should be trouble-free on the first operating session.

The first run on phase 1 of the MRL N scale layout took place around six months after starting the joinery when I ran a close replica of the Amtrak 'Empire Builder' over the first phase of the N scale MRL 4th Sub Division line from Missoula Yard, through DesMet Junction, around the peninsula to the base of the helix. The journey was completed by traversing the hidden return line along the back of the wall baseboards to the off-stage reverse loop and on to the main line, bypassing Missoula Yard once again, as if it had just travelled from the east, leaving the third subdivision track to enter the fourth again. This continuous run permitted demonstration running and the simple restaging of trains after a serious operating session.

During its maiden voyage, the train did not derail and completed its journey without anything more than a few clicks over rail joiners. I noted which ones would benefit from a little attention with emery cloth to remove burrs after rail cutting, and then continued the initial test run with a coal drag and a intermodal stack train. There is no doubt that the trains have a vote on your work and some locomotives required fine tuning to improve performance, including the application of liquid traction tyres called 'Bull Frog Snot' on some wheels to improve the adhesion on the gradients! For the following weeks, fine tuning and playing trains was the order of the day, bedding things in, programming DCC decoders to match locomotive speed for consisting and checking anything that was running less than satisfactorily.

The Folkestone East theme was also brought on line during the time of writing, with operations from one staging yard to the other to test the track and rolling stock. That too saw a number of weeks of fine tuning work to locomotives, EMUs and rolling stock.

Both the MRL 4th Sub layout and Folkestone East are a long way from their 'golden spike' ceremonies and much work remains to be done, which is outside the scope of this book, but is a further and important facet of layout construction. That work includes the building of the scenery for south-west Montana and the Kent coast, ballasting and detailing the track, building important railway structures such as signalling, the huge (and curved) trestle bridge that spans Fish Creek at milepost 165 on the 4th Sub line, the distinctive signal box at Folkestone East and the portal of Martello Tunnel.

Still, I have to show how to finish the layout with neat backdrops with trees, sky and clouds, install view blockers to enhance the driving experience, design the lighting, fit neat fascias and complete much work to turn the layout into a beautifully presented model. That is to be followed by devising operating plans, timetables and operational 'wrinkles', such as a hot-box detector random-fault card system to make operating the layouts much more fun and interesting. This is where railway modelling becomes interesting for many modellers, turning 'Plywood Parkway' into a fully scenic and operationally accurate model. But like the construction of the basic structure, it's going to take a little time! I plan for it to be a fascinating and satisfying journey, just like the one I have described here.

INDEX

RELATED TITLES
FROM CROWOOD

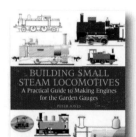

Building Small Steam Locomotives
A Practical Guide to Making Engines for the Garden Gauges

PETER JONES

ISBN 978 1 84797 029 9

224pp, over 300 illustrations

Detailing and Modifying Ready-to-Run Locomotives in OO Gauge
Volume 1: British Diesel & Electric Locomotives, 1955–2008

GEORGE DENT

ISBN 978 1 84797 093 0

192pp, over 350 illustrations

Detailing and Modifying Ready-to-Run Locomotives in OO Gauge
Volume 2: British Steam Locomotives, 1948–1968

GEORGE DENT

ISBN 978 1 84797 145 6

192pp, over 400 illustrations

Digital Command Control for Railway Modellers

NIGEL BURKIN

ISBN 978 1 84797 020 6

192pp, over 400 illustrations

Practical Garden Railways

PETER JONES

ISBN 978 1 86126 833 4

224pp, over 350 illustrations

In case of difficulty in ordering, contact the Sales Manager:

The Crowood Press Ltd
Ramsbury
Wiltshire
SN8 2HR
UK

Tel: 44 (0) 1672 520320
enquiries@crowood.com
www.crowood.com